MW01178753

Bible studies on

Joseph & Judah

Mark Vander Hart

Reformed Fellowship, Inc.
3363 Hickory Ridge Ct. SW
Grandville, MI 49418

©2008 Reformed Fellowship, Inc.
Printed in the United States of America
All rights reserved

For information:
Reformed Fellowship, Inc.
3363 Hickory Ridge Ct. SW
Grandville, MI 49418
Phone: 616.532.8510
Web: reformedfellowship.net
Email: sales@reformedfellowship.net

Book design by Jeff Steenholdt

ISBN 978-0-9793677-8-6

Contents

Young Joseph is Both Loved and Hated

Read Genesis 37:2–11

Introduction

We turn here to the stories that will revolve mainly around
Joseph and also Judah. But again, we must be alert to what
God is doing to advance His cause and His Kingdom in and
through Joseph and Judah. The Bible does not give us
interesting biographies of the "good guys" and the "bad guys."
The Biblical story is tracing a covenant line that will draw
our attention always forward to the coming of the Lord
Jesus Christ, His Person and work, and the coming of the
Kingdom of God.

There are two things to notice about the opening verses of
Genesis 37. First of all, Jacob is brought back into the story
after we have read through the "account of Esau (that is,
Edom)," which occupied Genesis 36. Esau and his
descendants, the Edomites, will occupy land to the south of
the Dead Sea. But Jacob will occupy Canaan, the Promised
Land, where his own father Isaac had lived throughout
his life. Second, note that in verse 2, we have the last of the
"accounts" (or "generations") of the book of Genesis.
We met the first one in Genesis 2:4, the "account
(or generations) of the heavens and the earth."
These several accounts had given textual shape to the
book of Genesis as matters continued to narrow down to
focus the readers' attention upon the family of Jacob,

the people of Israel. These accounts provide a name, and then tell us "what happened" to him and his family. So, we will see Jacob in the Biblical story here, but attention will soon focus on Joseph and Judah and how God will use these two sons. Judah, we remember, is the fourth son of Jacob, while Joseph is the "younger son," the son of Jacob's favorite wife Rachel.

What do we mean here in saying, "younger son"? First of all, we recall that Joseph is in fact the oldest son of Rachel and Jacob. Rachel had been unable to have children for some time, and this had caused her great distress (see Gen. 30:1–8). Yet in time, "God remembered Rachel," she gives birth to her firstborn son, Joseph ("may He add;" Gen. 30:22–24). In relationship to the other half-brothers, Joseph is the youngest son. Some day he would, in God's marvelous plan, become the powerful ruler of Egypt, and his brothers would serve him (cf. Gen. 25:23).

Genesis 37:2–11 divides into two parts: the first part focuses on Jacob's love for Joseph, while the second part reveals the message that comes through two dreams. Both sections in these verses have one thing in common: the hatred the sons of Jacob have against their own half-brother, Joseph.

The Father's Love, the Brothers' Hate (37:2–4)

Jacob is an old man at this point, and he loves the "son of his old age," whose status is enhanced by the fact that Joseph is the son of his beloved wife Rachel (now deceased; see Gen. 35:19). Jacob loves him more than all of his older sons, a fact not unnoticed by those sons, something that is not lost on them and their attitude. We meet Joseph now, after his birth notice, when he is a teenager, a boy 17 years of age.

There is an earlier account of a parent showing favoritism to a particular child. Jacob's own father Isaac had loved Esau more because of the tasty wild game that Esau could catch, prepare and serve as food. Jacob, on the other hand, had been loved by his mother. Those dynamics of favoritism had let loose in the family some very unhealthy things. Now Jacob shows his own love to this younger son, Joseph.

He makes it blatantly evident by the special coat that he prepared for Joseph. Some translations have called it a "coat of many colors," but this is not likely the translation. The same phrase of description is given to the kind of garment that Tamar, the daughter of King David, would wear later (see 2 Sam. 13:18). Some have suggested that the coat was ornamented with long sleeves and would indicate a person of royal position. While we cannot be dogmatic here, it is likely that Joseph was "dressed like a king," and that by his own father. And Joseph is certainly not in the position of being the oldest son: there are ten older brothers ahead of him! Brotherly jealousy and resentments are somewhat understandable.

But there are other reasons that the text gives for why the brothers hate Joseph. While he helped out by working with his half-brothers, who were the sons of the concubines, he brings back a "bad report" about his brothers to his father. Our culture generally hates a snitch, a tattletale, but it is not clear if that is the way we should read and hear this story. On the other hand, we also value the "whistle-blower" who calls the dishonest to public account. In either case, the exposure of the brothers' evil (whatever it may have been) is something they hate. Civil conversations between the brothers and Joseph were no more (verse 4).

"I Had a Dream…and Another Dream" (37:5–11)

The two dreams are further reasons for the brothers' hatred against Joseph. Even father Jacob is made thoughtful about what this all means. Dreams will play a significant role in the entire Joseph story (cf. the dreams of the two royal prisoners, and the dreams of the Pharaoh).

Joseph's two dreams basically have the same message. In each, something that represented Joseph himself receives the bowing down of the other objects that represent his family members. Joseph's sheaf stands, and his brothers sheaves bow to his sheaf. In the second dream, the celestial "governors," the sky rulers—the sun, the moon, and the stars—bow down to Joseph. If God had sent such dreams to Joseph, then God is saying that Joseph will someday be a great ruler. Jacob had honored his son with his love and with a special coat. Now it appears that God will greatly honor him as well in the future. There are two reactions in the family: the brothers only use the dreams of Joseph to fuel their hatred and jealousy, while father Jacob is perplexed, perhaps wondering if things are now beginning to get out of hand, or thinking that Joseph's dreams may have only exaggerated the honored position that Jacob had given him. It is one thing to claim that Joseph will rule in the future, but will Jacob himself actually bow down to Joseph? Jacob does not forget this: he pondered these things in his heart.

Mary, the mother of our Lord Jesus, will do a similar thing later at the birth of Christ. Read Luke 2:19 and 2:51. Pondering and meditating upon the revelation of God is, in fact, the attitude of a good, submissive disciple. A good disciple will take the revelation of God and store it in his heart, like seed that falls on good soil. Such a disciple can then produce a bumper crop for God's Kingdom. Is this what will happen with Jacob? Jacob ponders these things, but his sons do a slow simmer of hatred.

Covenant Sons That are Like Their "Father"

We begin to feel at this point that we have been here before. In a covenant home where the true God should be known, loved, worshiped, and honored, we find instead the things of the ancient Serpent, the devil, coming to expression. Jesus told the Jews the truth, and that truth sets anyone free (John 8:31). But the Jews rejected both the message and the Messenger, Jesus. Yet, they claimed that they remained Abraham's children. Jesus' reply is telling: "You belong to your father the devil...he was a murderer from the beginning, not holding to the truth, for there is no truth in him. When he lies, he speaks his native language, for he is a liar and the father of lies" (John 8:44).

Spiritually, Cain acted like the devil when he murdered his brother and then lied to God. A similar thing will happen in Genesis 37 when the brothers of Joseph will wish to kill him and then lie to their own father. The power of evil is great, even in the lives of people who should know and live according to the Kingdom of God.

Jesus also faced lies and plots of murder. Yet, the grace of God is greater than all the sin and guilt that exist in this world. God reveals His perfect will so that we might live by it. The wicked will reject God's will because they act according to their nature. By nature we all hate God, His Son, His message, and we hate our neighbors as well! This does not stop our great God: He works even through human wickedness to bring His perfect designs to pass. Acts 2:22ff. and Acts 3:18 (cf. Acts 4:28) tell us that the Jews handed over God's righteous Son, the Lord Jesus Christ, to wicked men, even after God had accredited Jesus in the presence of all. But it was precisely through these actions, wicked in their motive and method, that God worked out the salvation of all His elect through the Cross and the resurrection. This is grace: God's riches established at Christ's expense. Indeed, God moves in a mysterious way!

Points to Ponder and Discuss

1. In the ancient world, it was commonly understood that the gods could communicate their wills to people by means of dreams. In fact, God had appeared to Jacob in a very important dream at Bethel (Gen. 28:10ff.). If this is so, why did Joseph's brothers not understand these two dreams in a similar way? In other words, if dreams are from God, then the family must submit to God's plan and not "hate the messenger" (Joseph), right? What does this suggest about the spirituality of Joseph's brothers? What reaction do modern church members have to God's revelation today, especially when it "steps on our toes"?

2. God made His plan known for Joseph by means of dreams. Does God still make known His will today by means of dreams? (Yes, there are people today who profess the Christian faith and who attach significance to dreams!). How do we understand Hebrews 1:1–3 in this regard?

3. Joseph's brothers hated him. How is it possible for brothers who are raised in the same "Christian" home to hate their own flesh-and-blood to such extent as we see in this chapter? What can parents do when they see such hatred beginning to show itself?

4. We see a gradual escalation in the levels of bitterness that arise in the sons of Jacob. Apparently none of them try to check this hatred and stop it. There is such a thing as "mob violence" and "mob (or group) hatred." How does this appear today? Where have you seen or experienced this yourself? Can "coffee cup gossip" about certain people be a subtle form of such hatred? How do cliques, closed circles of friends, become a negative thing in school or in a congregation?

5. Jacob's favoritism to Joseph plays a role in the brothers' growing hatred against Joseph. Is this then a story about "bad parenting," or is it a story about the covenant seed, that is, the family line that carries God's redemptive plan? What is this "covenant seed" like in Genesis 37? Are they being influenced perhaps by the ways of the Canaanites?

6. Commentators are divided in their evaluation of Joseph's personality in Genesis 37. Some see him as a proud and arrogant snitch, one who did not handle the message of the dreams in a responsible way. Others see him as a faithful and dutiful son, one who obeys his father, knows what is evil and will not stand for it (even in his brothers). How do you read this part of the story, and why? In the end, is the focus on the person of Joseph, or should we ask how the Spirit of Jesus is working here in the people and events of this story?

Lesson 2

Jacob's Sons Attempt to Rid Themselves of Joseph

Read Genesis 37:12–36

Introduction

In the opening verses of Genesis 37 we are given a glimpse into the attitudes that lived in the household of aging Jacob. He has children from four different women, two wives and two maidservants. But Jacob loves the firstborn of his beloved wife Rachel, and he does not hide that fact in any way. The text makes clear that a series of events (e.g., a special coat, two dreams, etc.) cause brother hatred to escalate against Joseph. Yet, the clear message that comes through is that some royal role belongs to young Joseph. Father Jacob seems to want it, and, if dreams come from God, then this royalty appears to have divine approval as well.

Jacob Sends Joseph on a Mission (37:12–14)

Joseph's brothers take their father's flocks to graze near Shechem (the city where the massacre had occurred in Gen. 34). The household of Jacob is semi-nomadic; that is, they lived in tents in a particular area as long as enough water and grazing area exist for the flocks and herds. If necessary, a nomad like Jacob would move around, or move his flocks, to any place where supplies of water and grazing fields were available. Jacob has been living near Hebron; his sons must take the herds to an area in central Canaan, just over 50 miles (over 80 kilometers) to the north.

Jacob sends Joseph to check on the well-being (*shalom*) of his brothers and the flocks. Interesting irony: earlier in verse 4 the text notes that Joseph's brothers could not speak a "kind word" (literally, *shalom*) to him. We wonder whether it is possible that Jacob does not know how intense the hatred is by his sons against Joseph. Could that fact have simply gone over his head? It is hard to believe that Jacob is completely unaware of the brothers' intense dislike of Joseph. If he is aware of it, why does he send young Joseph to the brothers? Or is it the case that Jacob is, in fact, aware of family friction (normal, isn't it?), but that he believes his sons would never do anything harmful or malicious to Joseph? In any case, he sends young Joseph to find them.

He Came to His Own, but... (37:14–20)

The brothers have, in fact, moved on from Shechem to Dothan, almost 15 miles (about 24 kilometers) north of Shechem. An unnamed man helps Joseph find the brothers, and they in turn see him coming from a distance. Although they do not have binoculars, apparently Joseph comes to them wearing the special coat that his father had made for him. This coat was only one of the reasons that the sons of Jacob hate Joseph. What should catch our attention is the fact that his mere appearance causes their hatred to flare up. Verse 18: "But they saw him in the distance, and before he reached them, they plotted to kill him." Joseph does not have to say a word to his brothers before they have murderous thoughts come out. One does not have to pinch or probe deeply at all in the souls of these brothers for there to be an eruption of murderous scheming. With sneering sarcasm, they call him a "master of dreams, the dreamer," thinking that by killing him they could snuff out any prospect of his dreams coming to fulfillment. Clearly they do not believe that the dreams are from God.

Reuben Plans to Rescue Joseph (37:21-24)

Reuben, the eldest brother and thus the "one in charge," persuades them not to kill Joseph for the moment, but only throw him into an empty cistern (his first "prison"). Reuben wants to pull them back from personal blood-guilt and rescue Joseph later. But Reuben leaves the area for a while. Joseph is stripped of his special coat, that hated symbol of the father's special love. If it is possible that Joseph was not sure of what his brothers thought of him before, there cannot be any doubt now. At this point, Joseph could only wonder if they were leaving him to die of hunger and thirst, or if they would actively take his life. He would cry out from that cistern for mercy, but his brothers would turn a deaf ear to his cries.

"Let's Make a Deal" (37:25-28)

It's time for lunch, and the brothers eat together. Joseph gets nothing. This sets us up for a great irony later on when the brothers would stand in Egypt, "hat in hand" so to speak, asking Joseph for food because of the great famine that would strike the land. But that is later. There are more ironies to come.

Canaan is strategically located as a place where several trade routes exist between Egypt and Mesopotamia. We are not surprised to read that a trading caravan is spotted on its way to Egypt. The identity of these traders may be confusing to some readers, as well as who sold whom. The explanation offered here is that "Ishmaelite" and "Midianite" are basically interchangeable terms. Both Ishmael and Midian are children of Abraham (see Gen. 25:1ff.). It may be that Ishmaelite came to be the more general term, while Midianite was a more specific term (cf. the use of terms "Arab" and "Iraqi," or "German" and "Bavarian" to illustrate the general and the specific identifications).

When these traveling merchants are spotted, it is Judah who comes up with the idea to sell Joseph. To him and his brothers, this seems to be a "win-win" solution: we don't actually kill Joseph, but instead we get some cash out of selling him. In other words, he is out of our life forever, plus we get some pocket change!

Joseph is sold for 20 pieces of silver. Later, in the law of Moses, a male slave (between 5 and 20 years of age), specially dedicated to the Lord, was valued at 20 shekels. According to the Hammurabi law code, this was the price of male slaves in the ancient Near East at that time (prices for slaves would rise over the centuries, of course). Joseph would later describe this event as being sold into Egypt, clearly against his will (see Gen. 40:15 and 45:4, 5).

Torn and Blood-Stained Clothing (37:29–34)

Reuben returns to his brothers, only to find young Joseph gone, now in chains and on his way to Egypt. Reuben tears his clothes as a sign of his grief. His plan to spare Joseph's life has now come to nothing. Reuben did not have the courage to stand up to his murder-plotting brothers. He did not rebuke them firmly for their plans, and now the result is the loss of Joseph. Reuben must now, probably with great reluctance, go along with the clever strategy of his brothers to deceive his own father.

But there is more. The brothers take Joseph's special coat, kill a goat and use its blood to stain the coat. When they confront their father with this coat, their words are clever in the sense that they say nothing that is contrary to fact. "Examine it to see whether it is your son's robe." They do not even use his name "Joseph." He is "your son," not, "our brother." Jacob recognizes it and then makes the conclusion that the brothers had hoped he would make. "It's Joseph's coat; a wild (literally, 'evil') animal has eaten him."

There is an irony here: Jacob had used goat meat and goat's skins (clothes) earlier to deceive his father Isaac (Gen. 27:16) to obtain the blessing. Now another goat dies to provide the blood to deceive another father, but this time the father is Jacob! Jacob now tears his own clothes as a sign of grief.

Grief Carried to the Grave (37:34–35)

Those who grieve go through various stages of mood. When one loses a precious family member or beloved friend, you know these moods of grief. There is perhaps denial, anger, depression, a general melancholy. The passage of time may help, but usually some kind of emotional scar remains. We need to work through this grief, and the presence of family and friends can help. Jacob's children surround him to support him, comfort him, and help him through his understandable grief. This old man Jacob has lost the beloved son of his favorite wife. He has seen many blessings from God over the years, but now he refuses to accept anyone's comforting words or gestures. Jacob is prepared to carry this grief into his grave, the realm of the dead.

Sold as a Slave (37:36)

Genesis 37 ends on a sad, ominous note: Joseph is sold in Egypt to a very high ranking official of the court of Pharaoh. We will say more about this man Potiphar in a later lesson. Psalm 105:17 notes that Joseph has been reduced to slavery. He has moved at the beginning of this chapter from being the beloved and favored son of his father to utter humiliation. Such a descent into slavery was at the hands of his blood brothers! And yet, the fact that the man who purchased him was an official of Pharaoh carries rich possibilities. At least Joseph is not sold into obscurity, to slave away his young life for a few years and then die unknown in some remote village of Egypt. The last verse of Genesis 37 tantalizes the reader and sets us up for the further developments of Genesis 39.

Since nothing comes to us by chance, but everything by God's fatherly hand, we know that some divine plan is being worked out. But God does not appear to any of the characters, neither to Joseph nor to Jacob, to inform them of what is happening. Other Biblical characters may have reassuring visits from God's angels or even a divine voice ("Don't be afraid!"), but such a visit or such a voice does not come forward here. We can only wonder what may have passed through Joseph's mind in these days, weeks, and months. His situation plummets from royal riches, so to speak, to wretched rags in this chapter. Did these kinds of questions nag at his soul: "Why did my own brothers do this to me?" "What kind of God do I serve?" "Is there no justice in this world?"

It is one thing to fall under difficult circumstances in life and see God's disciplinary hand as rightly there. But it is quite another thing to suffer for no apparent reason. And God remains silent. Can any human faith suffice then to hold onto God? If Joseph is to survive both spiritually and physically, then a power and strength greater than anything Joseph has must be with him. But such is God's grace.

Points to Ponder and Discuss

1. How can we explain Jacob's decision to send Joseph off to visit his brothers? Is Jacob completely unaware that his sons loathe Joseph? Do parents sometimes act "in denial" about realities that anyone else can see? Or, can parents simply fail to pick up on the important personal life clues that close family members can give?

2. This family of Jacob is the church! Or is it? What explanation can we give to the fact that the desire to kill Joseph— or at least be rid of him—has the overwhelming support of most of Jacob's sons? We will see something very similar when Pharisees, people who said that all Israelites must live pure and holy lives, will actively plot to kill the Lord Jesus Christ. How can such murderous hatred exist among people who profess something else?

3. Read Exodus 21:16 and Deuteronomy 24:7 (cf. Deut. 23:15). Stealing property is an economic crime, but kidnapping and selling human beings was a capital crime.
   What is the difference between being a "servant" who works off a debt, on the one hand, and the kind of selling of people condemned in the law of God, on the other hand? Can human beings ever be viewed as property?

4. The movie "Amazing Grace" tells the story of the British Christian leader, William Wilberforce, who labored to rid the British Empire of slavery in the 19th century.
   What kind of slavery existed historically in the United States? What evils were let loose by such slavery? Why was it defended even by some Christians? Does such trafficking in human beings continue to this day?

5. The blood-stained coat convinces Jacob that Joseph
   is dead. His grief is quite understandable, is it not?
   Yet he refuses to be comforted. Could he wonder how his
   sons could have ever found this coat in all the
   countryside of Canaan? By refusing the comfort of his
   children, is it possible that Jacob may harbor a sneaking
   suspicion that somehow, somewhere, his own children
   were involved in the death of Joseph? Could the sons
   of Jacob pretend also to mourn? Many issues
   remain unresolved...

6. Look over Genesis 37 again. Is God ever mentioned in
   this chapter? How is God working in these sad events?
   What providences happen in this story that will work out
   a good result, even if it is very hard to see it at this point
   in the story?

Lesson 3

Judah Begins to Live in Canaan

Read Genesis 38:1–11

Introduction

It is puzzling perhaps to have this chapter placed in the Bible where it is. Genesis 37 ends with Joseph being sold to Potiphar, and Genesis 39:1 resumes the story account of Joseph. Yet the very fact that Genesis 39:1 is written as it is strongly suggests that the Biblical writer here "knows what he is doing." God the Holy Spirit wants the story of Judah, Tamar, and the birth of their two sons to say something about Jacob's family (cf. Gen. 37:2) and tie that in with Joseph's going down to Egypt. Any ideas come to your mind as to why this chapter is placed here by the Holy Spirit?

Judah Chooses Canaanite Friends and Family (38:1–2)

Judah had played an important role in what had happened to Joseph in Genesis 37. It was Judah who suggested that Joseph not be killed but rather sold (Gen. 37:26, 27). Now the story returns to focus its lens on what happens in the life of Judah. What we read in the opening verses of Genesis 38 is ominous: some time soon after Joseph was sold to traveling merchants, Judah moves away from his family. We are not told why. There does not seem to be any family discord. After all, later on he will join his other brothers in going to Egypt to get food during the famine.

In any case, the thoughtful reader of this text detects some not so subtle changes taking place. Earlier in Genesis, it was

clear that Isaac and Jacob had to have wives who were
not Canaanite. Rebekah, Rachel, and Leah all came from
the broader family circle back in Haran. Esau's Hittite
wives, on the other hand, had been a source of grief to Isaac
and Rebekah.

But concern for whom Judah marries does not appear in
this story. Judah moves into a Canaanite area and acquires
a Canaanite friend, Hirah of Adullam. Furthermore, he
marries a Canaanite woman, a daughter of Shua (or Bathshua).
Incidentally, the places and persons in this story anticipate
elements later on with King David: Adullam is a village
within tribal Judah's territory; Bathshua is similar sounding
to Bathsheba; David has a daughter named Tamar...but we
are getting ahead of ourselves.

Judah has a Canaanite wife and a circle of Canaanite friends.
It is not a great stretch of imagination to believe that
Canaanite values, a pagan world-view, were also
surrounding and influencing Judah. He does not seem
distressed by his new environment as righteous Lot was
disturbed when he lived in wicked Sodom (see 2 Peter 2:7, 8).
Of course, wickedness is not merely around us: it is also
within us. Judah also was involved in the plunder of
Shechem and the selling of Joseph. Still, Judah's move into
Canaan is more than simply a physical move. It suggests
something spiritually more dangerous.

My Three Sons (38:3–10)

Judah and his Canaanite wife have three sons (Er, Onan,
and Shelah), apparently in rather quick succession. As they
grow up in Judah's home, Joseph meanwhile has to deal
with sexual temptation and imprisonment, with only the
Lord as his aid. The Bible tells us that Judah obtained a
wife for his firstborn son Er. This wife is apparently a
Canaanite by the name of Tamar. Judah arranges this
marriage, something that is not unknown in other Biblical

stories and in the culture of that time. As we watch this story unfold, Judah will come across as a "take charge" kind of guy, a father figure who actively arranges things in his family.

The text does not waste words in ending Er's life. He is so wicked that the Lord ends his life. "Er erred," writes Gordon Wenham (*Genesis 16–50*, p. 366). Interestingly, in the Hebrew language, if you reverse the letters of the name *Er*, it creates the word that means *wicked*. But what was his evil? We are not told. We could pause for a moment and reflect on the quality of Judah's spiritual direction to his family, but the text does not make that a concern for us. Judah's reaction to his son's death is not recorded either. Jacob was grieved by the loss of Joseph. Judah's loss of Er is met with textual silence.

Judah tells the second son, Onan, to take the widow Tamar and "fulfill your duty to her as a brother-in-law" to produce an heir. This was an ancient practice designed to maintain the family line of the dead brother. The practice has become known as "levirate marriage" (*levir* is Latin for "brother-in-law"). Perhaps Onan calculates the possibilities: if the dead Er has no son, then only Onan and the other brother, Shelah, can divide the inheritance between them. But if Er has a son (through Onan and Tamar), then the firstborn would receive a substantial portion of the inheritance, thus diminishing what Onan would get. So, to prevent Tamar from becoming pregnant, Onan interrupts the sexual act and spills his semen on the ground. The net effect, therefore, is to use Tamar for his sexual pleasure, but he refuses the obligation to produce a son. This now becomes a case of incest, which would be clearly forbidden in the law of Moses (see Lev. 18:16). Onan thus is guilty of greed and deception as well as adultery by refusing to produce a son for his dead brother Er. The Lord, who searches all hearts and minds, executes Judah's second son. What must Judah think now? What thoughts pass through Tamar's heart as she observes these events around her? She has watched as two wicked sons of Judah die, and she is still without children.

Keeping the Name Alive (Deut. 25:5–10)

One issue that runs throughout Genesis 38 is that of childlessness and the highly irregular way in which that issue is resolved. Earlier we referred to "levirate marriage," a practice that the law of Moses would regulate. Read Deuteronomy 25:5–10. As we noted above, a man could not marry his sister-in-law. The exception for this came in the case of the brother who died without a son. The dead man's brother could take the widow as his wife. The purpose for this is explicit in Deuteronomy 25:6, "The first son she bears shall carry on the name of the dead brother so that his name shall not be blotted out in Israel."

The living brother might refuse this duty, and presumably another brother could step forward to accept this responsibility. If the brother declined this duty, the widow could appeal to the larger community (city elders). If their attempts at persuasion fall on deaf ears, then came the sandal ceremony (a sandal is taken off), coupled with the dishonoring event of being spit in the face. At least the poor chap was not executed! But his own family would gain a bad reputation that could last for years, acquiring the name, "Family of the Unsandaled."

This practice comes back before us (with some variations) in Ruth 4:1–12. The story is well-known. Boaz, a worthy Judean, is challenged by Ruth in Ruth 3 to marry her (on behalf of Naomi). Boaz is a near relative, a kinsman-redeemer. God designed the role of kinsman-redeemer to be that in which a relative would protect the poor, secure the land, and execute justice. Boaz knows that there is a relative who is closer to

Elimelech, Naomi's dead husband. This unnamed relative is challenged to buy Naomi's land, and he is willing to do so. But when told that Ruth the Moabite widow is part of the bargain, he backs out, claiming that he fears endangering his own inheritance. Apparently, the unnamed redeemer in Ruth 4 was afraid that if he had only one son, that son would receive not only all of Elimelech's possessions, but also his own property as well. In any case, Boaz is willing to take a risk and marry Ruth for the sake of Elimelech and Naomi's future in terms of family name and land preserved.

Thus we see that Deuteronomy 25:5–10 is not an odd law of God at all. Rather, it had a very deliberate "redemptive" purpose. Keeping a name alive through children provided a way for God's people to occupy and hold property in the Promised Land. Seed (children) and land were the "pillar promises" that Abraham, Isaac, and Jacob had repeatedly heard as gospel promises. Nothing must frustrate that!

When we come back to the story in Genesis 38, we note that Onan would prefer to see his dead brother Er remain childless, quite likely so that he might gain a greater inheritance. Later on in Israel, refusing your duty as a brother-in-law such behavior meant sandal-removing, spit in the face, and a bad family nickname. But for Onan, it meant death.

Jesus Christ, God's eternal and natural Son, was made like us in every way, but without sin (Heb. 2:14; 4:15). By becoming our Brother, Jesus became responsible to carry out the role of Kinsman-Redeemer. He protects His poor family (the elect brothers and sisters), He secures their inheritance, and He rights all wrongs by executing justice. When Adam, God's first human son, defaulted and failed, God sent His own Son, who never fails us. The church is not left a forlorn widow, but she is redeemed in divine love by Christ, who paid the ultimate price to secure the church as His own Bride.

Judah Sends Tamar Away (38:11)

Judah had arranged Tamar to be Er's wife initially. But now Judah does something quite unusual: he dismisses her from his family circle. Tamar is called "his daughter-in-law" in verse 11, please note. Of course, Judah holds out hope for the future. Once Shelah, the third son, is old enough for marriage, he can rise to the occasion and produce a son for Er. But what is more than unusual, even inappropriate, was for Judah to send Tamar away to her father's house. By marrying Er, Tamar had entered Judah's family. She was no longer under the authority of her own father, but she was now very much a part of Judah's household.

Judah in fact is deceiving Tamar. He thinks to himself, "Shelah may die as well." Therefore, why would he ever give Tamar to Shelah? Judah appears to blame Tamar somehow for the death of Er and Onan. Is she "bad luck"? Is she some kind of jinx to his sons? Judah appears to be the kind of father who is blind to his own sons' wickedness, but he is willing to blame the Canaanite woman. Therefore, by telling Tamar to wait in her father's house for Shelah to grow older, Judah is not being wholly honest. Judah treats Tamar like a pawn. By telling her to wait for Shelah, Tamar is not free to marry anyone else. She is consigned to a "no man's land." The problem is that Judah is shirking his duties, and even more importantly, Judah's line is in danger.

By entitling this lesson, "Judah begins to live in Canaan," we indicate much more than that he moved away from his brothers geographically. Judah and his sons are sinking deeper into Canaanite culture and pagan depravity. Of course, Judah showed something of this even earlier. But if Judah stays in Canaan, then humanly speaking, the future is dark and grim. To think that David and, later, Jesus Christ come from this household! Some radical and powerful grace from God must intervene.

Points to Ponder and Discuss

1. The Lord strikes Er and Onan dead for their wickedness. What do we learn about the consequences of sin? In this regard think of the Flood and the end of the cities of Sodom and Gomorrah. Why is God's justice so immediate in the case of Judah's sons?

2. Judah seems to be almost blind to the reason for his sons' deaths. He appears to blame Tamar. How is it possible for parents to be blind or maybe oblivious to sinfulness in their children? Do some parents have the attitude of "my child would never do that"? Have they perhaps forgotten what they were like when they were younger? What does the psalmist mean when he prays, "Remember not the sins of my youth" (Ps. 25:7)?

3. How aware does Judah seem to be to his own calling before God? Does he see himself as distinctive in this world in terms of his identity and his covenantal responsibility? Or, does he just want to have a "nice life"?

4. The Sadducees refer back to this practice of brothers marrying a widow of a dead brother. See Luke 20:27ff. How do Sadducees understand this practice? Are they mocking it in the case they tell Jesus? What does our Lord teach about marriage in the age to come?

5. The practice of *levirate marriage* was intended to preserve a name alive and thus the claim to the *land*. Where do Christians today get their *name*, i.e., their identity? Where is our land, i.e., our inheritance in the Promised Land? Who holds that name and land for believers today and preserves them safe for believers? (Hint: think of Rev. 3:12, of baptism and the coming new creation)

6. How difficult was it for Lot and his family when they moved into Sodom? How difficult does it appear to be spiritually for Judah and his family when he moves into Canaan? How difficult is it today for Christians as we live in this world (although we are not of this world)? What role do the Christian church, Christian education, and other Christian organizations have to play in equipping God's people for life in this world?

Lesson 4

Tamar's Younger Son "Breaks Through" to Secure Judah's Line

Read Genesis 38:12–30

Introduction

This chapter is a sordid story that reveals a most unseemly side in Judah and his family. He has wicked sons, so wicked that the Lord Himself removes them through death.
Then Judah removes Tamar, implying by his actions (and thoughts) that she must be somehow responsible for the death of Er and Onan. But there is more to Tamar, and this chapter reveals how she acts in a "more righteous" way than Judah. Her actions result in the answer for the grand problem in this chapter, namely, the threat of childlessness.

Tamar Deceives Judah (38:12–14)

Time passes, and another member of Judah's family dies, namely, his wife Bathshua. Perhaps we feel some sympathy for this man. Just as Naomi will later lose both her husband and two sons, so now Judah has lost two sons and his wife. His son Shelah remains.

Tamar has been living with her own father since Judah sent her away following the death of Onan. Up to this point, Tamar has been quite passive in the story: her marriage had been arranged by Judah, and it is Judah who removed her from the family circle. We have not heard her speak in the text. But her clothing tells a story. Judah comes to the end of his mourning period, but Tamar continues to wear her widow's clothing (verse 14). We do not know how long a widow might wear such clothing in that culture. In her case, it may very well be her way of saying that she still belongs to Judah's household, a widow of one husband, but waiting for Shelah to reach the age when he could produce a son for his dead brother Er.

For Judah, life should resume some normalcy. With his friend Hirah, Judah goes into the hill country to participate in the shearing of sheep. Normally, that would be a time of partying, and so it may have been a time to help Judah move beyond his recent grievous losses.

Tamar now takes action. After she is told about Judah's movements, she disguises herself by putting on clothing that suggested she was a prostitute, veils herself, and waits at a public spot. She is no fool as she realizes that Judah has been less than honest with her. She had been promised Shelah as a husband, but Judah never issues the call for Tamar to come back to his family circle. In effect, Tamar was deceived, and now she will deceive Judah.

Judah Visits a "Prostitute" (38:15–19)

Earlier we made the point that Judah had moved into Canaan, and Canaanite attitudes were influencing him. But Judah is not a helpless puppet, and he brings his own sinful nature with him as he settles in Canaan, marries a Canaanite, and establishes a strong friendship with a Canaanite. Although he is now a widower, Judah has no right to visit a prostitute. Loneliness may be what he feels, but it is no excuse for what he now does.

Tamar's actions also cause thoughtful readers to raise the eyebrow and shake their heads in disgust. True, she is not really becoming a prostitute as a career, but surely this trick—dressing up as a prostitute in order to have sexual relations with Judah—cannot be right. Can it?

In any case, Judah takes the proverbial bait. Spotting a "prostitute," he makes his approach, and these two consenting adults agree to the terms: she will get a young goat in exchange for sexual intimacy. But Judah is not in the habit of carrying a young goat around with him! Nor does he have enough money on him. This action thus appears to be a somewhat spontaneous act on Judah's part. He was not looking for a prostitute, but he quickly hatched a plan once he saw her along the road.

Tamar asks for a pledge, and she suggests a couple of very valuable, personal objects from Judah. The seal was a hollowed-out cylinder that would have had distinctive markings (or ornamentation) on it. Typically worn around the neck with a cord, it could be pressed upon soft clay to make a "signature." The staff (or scepter!) would likely have a carved or ornamented top as well. All this suggests that Judah is not a poor man, for a young goat would be cheap payment for his sexual tryst with a Canaanite prostitute. But to give away his seal and staff is comparable to giving away one's credit card or a checkbook! What was Judah thinking?

We also note in passing how clothing and a young goat play a role in deception. Jacob had dressed like Esau and served goat meat to his father. Judah and his brothers had killed a goat to spill its blood on Joseph's special coat. Now Tamar uses prostitute clothes to deceive Judah, who promises a young goat to the "prostitute."

The story moves quickly as both parties appear to get what they want. Verse 18 says that "he gave...slept with her...and she conceived." She resumes her posture as a widow by means of her clothing, but the readers all know that what Judah will soon learn: Tamar is pregnant!

The Joke is on Judah (38:20–23)

Judah wants to pay up. She needs to get the goat so that Judah can get his "credit cards" (the seal and the staff) back again. He is quick to fulfill this obligation while the obligation to Tamar (and thus to his own son Er) he does not simply neglect, he has no intention of keeping. His Adullamite friend takes the payment, and he asks around for the shrine prostitute (using a different word from that used in verse 15). An ordinary prostitute (e.g., Rahab) did not have as high a status in Canaanite society as did a shrine prostitute. To visit a shrine prostitute was a religious act, in fact a superstitious one, since it was thought that sexual relations with shrine prostitutes would make the gods bless your land: your crops and your livestock would receive fertility.

But there was no shrine prostitute around here, the locales report. She's gone! Now Judah is in a bind: he has his young goat, but he really would like his "credit cards" back. He's been "taken to the cleaners!"

Judah does not appear to blush much at all here. Yes, he's embarrassed by his loss but not by his sin. When you move into Canaan, the very real danger is that Canaan moves into you! Living in Canaan involves satisfying the sinful nature and its lusts, including visits to prostitutes, whether involved with shrines or not. If God does not intervene in this story, Judah is on the road to death.

Who is the Father Anyway? (38:24–26)

By the third month of Tamar's pregnancy, the word is out. Tamar is with child. But who is the father of the child? Tamar has patiently waited, dressed in her widow's clothes, waiting for the head of the house, Judah, to call her back to his family circle to be joined with Shelah, his only surviving son. That call to come back never comes. Judah and everyone else conclude that Tamar has been involved in illicit sexual activity, specifically, prostitution. On one level they are right: she had acted like a prostitute. Yes, but…Tamar had resorted to desperate means to secure something of great importance to her personally, no doubt, but even more important, her pregnancy will have great significance for the coming of the Kingdom of God.

Judah decrees the death penalty: death by fire for Tamar, a most extreme punishment. Later on in the law of Moses, if a priest's daughter was involved in prostitution, she had to die by fire (Lev. 21:9). At the same time, had the facts been fully known, since Tamar was technically betrothed to Shelah, the penalty for adultery was death by stoning (see Deut. 22:23–24). Capital crimes, striking as they do at fundamental matters, require capital punishment.

Tamar is arrested, no doubt by family members. But she has a final trump card to play. She produces Judah's seal and staff (his "credit cards"). Tamar clinches her defense argument with the statement, "I am pregnant by the man who owns these. Recognize these?" That question is similar to the one Judah and his brothers had asked father Jacob about Joseph's coat. One can only imagine how wide Judah's eyes became as he indeed recognized these personal items of identification. And perhaps he blushed deeply, for his sin has now been exposed.

But if Judah blushed, he did more than that. He also dismissed the case against Tamar. "She is more righteous than I," declares Judah. This statement may likely strike us as odd, even startling. Is Judah saying that Tamar's methods are acceptable, that the "end justifies the means"? That is not what Judah means, especially as he points to his own refusal to give Shelah in marriage to Tamar.

"Tamar is in the right" means that Tamar took the call to bear children seriously enough. Er and Onan were dead; Shelah is kept away. God had promised a "seed of the woman" that would crush the serpent's head. God had promised numerous descendants to Abraham, Isaac, and Jacob. But now Judah stood in the way. So, Tamar resorts to highly questionable and most unusual actions to secure a child in Judah's line. Judah says that, by comparison, Tamar is right while he was not right.

The Second Son "Breaks Through" (38:27–30)

It's twins…again! Rebekah in Genesis 25:24–26 had a "lively" pregnancy with twins who struggled in her womb. With Tamar, her twins "struggle" to be born first. The little infant hand of one emerges from the womb, and he is designated with a scarlet thread as the actual firstborn. His name is Zerah (meaning "scarlet" or "shining"), the ancestor of Achan. But then the second son emerges. He "breaks through" to everyone's surprise, and thus he is named Perez, "break through." As Ruth 4:18ff. shows, he is the ancestor of King David and thus of King Jesus Christ.

Gordon Wenham (Genesis 16–50, p. 370) observes that "this story, which at first sight seems so marginal to biblical history, records a vital link in saving history. Tamar, through her determination to have children, secured for Judah the honor of fathering both David and the Savior of the world." Jesus Christ is the ultimate Son who "breaks through" in a way that no one expected. The second and last Adam of history comes through for us. Once again, we stand amazed that God would move in a mysterious and gracious way for the salvation of His own. He uses even a Canaanite woman, Tamar, who was determined to have a son to maintain the line of Judah. Tamar will become a mother even of the Christ.

Points to Ponder and Discuss

1. I once was told by a long-time member of a church that he did not even know that this story was in the Bible. Why might that be the case? Is this chapter sometimes skipped in Bible reading around the family table? Have you heard many (or any) sermons preached on Genesis 38? What makes this chapter so uncomfortable for us?

2. Judah sees a prostitute, and he desires to have sexual relations with her. In the Lord's Prayer, we pray, "Lead us not into temptation." What is temptation? How does it differ from divine testing? Who are our "sworn enemies that never stop attacking us"? See James 1; Heidelberg Catechism, Lord's Day 52, Q&A 127; Westminster Larger Catechism, Q&A 195; Westminster Shorter Catechism, Q&A 106.

3. Tamar is determined to have children. Could Tamar know about the divine promises in the covenant of grace, namely, that God would give both seed (children) and land? Or is she simply motivated by a maternal instinct, a natural desire to have children? Is there any way that we can tell from the Biblical text? How does God use and bless this desire to have children?

4. Judah wants Tamar burned for engaging, he believes, in prostitution. Most civil governments today in North America punish prostitution, but they no longer punish adultery or other acts carried out by "consenting adults." Should such things be punished (again) by the civil magistrates? Could such things be outlawed again? Or should Christians try only to change people's views and behaviors in these areas without a change in legislation?

5. We do not believe that the "end justifies the means." But are there ethical "grey areas"? What actually does "justify the means" that are used toward any particular end or goal?

6. Matthew 1 has a genealogy that leads to Christ's birth. What unusual women are in that list who are the mothers (ancestresses) of Jesus Christ? What unusual things do they do that serves or advances God's cause?

Lesson 5

Joseph is Tested in Egypt

Read Genesis 39

Introduction

Genesis 38 was a necessary chapter that fits perfectly in the story of Jacob's family. Joseph is chosen by God for some special purpose (to rule?), but his brothers sell him to merchants on the way to Egypt (Gen. 37). Then Judah moves away from his own family and settles in Canaan (in more ways than one). Canaanite culture and world-views threaten to swallow up Judah (and perhaps the rest of the family). Even Judah's family line is threatened until Tamar deceives her father-in-law in order to secure a child and thus raise up seed (and a name). Still, something must happen to move Jacob's family away from Canaan lest the church of God, Jacob's family, be lost among Canaanites. God has a great plan in mind, and Joseph will be the agent in that plan.

The Lord Blesses Joseph in Potiphar's House (39:1–6)

The text somewhat abruptly switches back to the Joseph story, basically picking up where it had left off at the end of chapter 37. Joseph is sold to an Egyptian official named Potiphar. He is described as "the captain of the guard," which suggests that Potiphar headed the security teams that surrounded the Pharaoh, a kind of leader of the Egyptian "secret service." Some have wondered whether there were Asiatics who were temporarily in charge of Egypt at this time, thus allowing Joseph to be well received in Egypt. However, the name "Potiphar" is Egyptian, and an Egyptian Pharaoh would not have employed a non-Egyptian to be his chief bodyguard.

In any case, there is a significant statement made in verse 2, and its truth is repeated in this chapter several times. "The Lord was with Joseph and he prospered." See verses 3, 21, and 23. Joseph is in the house of Potiphar at first, and then later he is in prison. But no matter where he is in the events of this chapter, the covenant God is with Joseph with a noticeable result: prosperity and blessing are experienced. This is a very important notice, because in some versions of telling this story, the accent or emphasis falls on "how Joseph resisted temptation." The suggestion is that Joseph's story in Genesis 39 is told to present first of all a model to us of "good Christian behavior." And the application would then be, "Go, and do likewise." While it is true that we certainly commend Joseph's response to his several situations, in Potiphar's home and later on in prison, the key to Joseph's "success" is the very presence of the covenant-making and covenant-keeping God. The Name of God used here is the one that will later be given to Moses at the burning bush (Exodus 3). That same God is not stranded in Canaan with Jacob's family, but He chooses in His grace to be with Joseph through everything. "The Lord was with Joseph"...and that will make all the difference!

What's more, the Lord's blessing upon Joseph is evident to his master Potiphar. While it is too much of a stretch to say that Potiphar becomes a true believer, we can say that the Egyptian official is convinced that the God of Joseph is with this young man, and that is a good thing. Joseph is given grace to hold on to this God, and his response is to take his responsibilities and duties seriously. This leads to a promotion for Joseph in the household of Potiphar. Literally, Potiphar puts everything into Joseph's "hand" (see verses 3, 4, 6, 8, 22, 23). Blessings begin to flow into the entire household (verse 5) "because of Joseph." The text says that these blessings could be seen in both the house and in the field. Did the birth rate pick up among Potiphar's servants?

Did his fields yield a bumper crop? The text is silent on these matters, and yet we are tantalized to wonder how the blessing of the Lord became physically evident to them.

Furthermore, the providence of God is such that this young, strong Hebrew is not sent out to work in the fields, but he is kept in the house where his abilities are put to work. Potiphar will trust him (much like father Jacob had trusted him) so that he will not be bothered with the details of the household: Joseph is in charge, and he knows what he is doing.

Joseph Flees Immorality (39:6–20)

Joseph is the son of a very attractive mother, Rachel. While we do not know what Jacob's physical appearance is like, we read in verse 6 that Joseph is both well-built and handsome. (Similar things will be said about David and Esther later on.) Keep in mind that he is still a young man, and he is all alone in terms of having no family around to help him, support him, or protect him. Even Daniel had his three friends in the court of Nebuchadnezzar, but Joseph is isolated in the sense that he has no community of like-minded believers around him.

He is thus prey to abuse by those in authority over him, and he catches the eye of his master's wife. The story reads like a modern TV soap opera, but the result is much happier than the silly soap opera. Yet Joseph will not have an easy time of it, and his faith and moral fiber will be sorely tested.

Joseph is a young and attractive man. This catches the eye of Mrs. Potiphar, and she desires an affair with him. "Lie with me!" she orders. This is not a one time incident: verse 10 tells us that her sexual invitations were a daily temptation to Joseph. Her lurid enticements were a kind of sexual harassment that was uninvited and unwanted. Scripture includes the speech of Joseph in verses 8–9 in which he lays out the reasons why he will not go to bed with Mrs. Potiphar. First of all, Joseph points out that he is placed in charge of everything in Potiphar's house. Humanly speaking, Joseph is at the top; only Potiphar's wife is off-limits to him. Secondly, and much more importantly, the adulterous affair that she wants with Joseph would be sin against God. Joseph not only knows God's will, he embraces it as his own. Adultery is a "wicked thing" in the eyes of God, and it brings misery to all who practice it.

Joseph's resistance to these enticements is no slight thing. As a servant, he does not have a lot of room to maneuver. It is not the case that he can quit his job and apply elsewhere. Is he going to go to a local court and file a complaint against this woman? Not likely! In a way he is trapped in the situation, and we may well imagine that the power of temptation for a virile young man, a servant no less, would be enormous, almost overwhelming. But, here is where the chapter's refrain (verses 2, 3, 21, 23) is so important to keep in mind: "the Lord was with him."

Potiphar's wife attempts to force him into adultery, but Joseph flees this immorality. He leaves behind his cloak in her hand. It is his clothing again that becomes important! His special coat, dipped in blood, suggested to Jacob that Joseph was dead. Now, in Mrs. Potiphar's hand, his coat is the evidence, the "smoking gun," to both servants and Potiphar alike that this "Hebrew slave" was not as good and virtuous as he seemed. Joseph is falsely accused, and the wicked woman's story seems believable indeed. When no one was around, this slave took advantage of the situation and tried to rape this poor, defenseless woman! She screamed when he had disrobed and attempted to rape her. Her screams (no tape recording available, of course) had frightened young Joseph to flee. This is her story to the other servants and to her husband.

What is interesting to notice, however, is that Potiphar, while very angry, does not kill Joseph. After all, since Joseph is nothing more than a servant, what rights would he have? And attempted rape against the official's wife? Death, of course! Yet God is with His people, even in the valley where death casts a shadow and where false accusations are made, and that is no different here. The fact that Potiphar does not kill Joseph but instead places him in a place for royal prisoners suggests at least two things: first, Potiphar must respect the accusation of his wife against Joseph at some level; he must "save face," both for himself and for her. So, he must do something. But second, one wonders if Potiphar does not fully believe his wife's story, and so, in his heart, he really has no desire to kill the young man Joseph. Potiphar must do something with him, but he spares his life. The jail for royal prisoners would not be the worst spot at all. God protects His own! Joseph survives another near death experience.

Joseph Prospers in Prison (39:20–23)

The story of Joseph in prison seems to be a repeat performance of what had happened earlier in Potiphar's house. Again, "the Lord was with him." The Spirit of Jesus Christ is so effective in the heart of Joseph that he applies himself and his God-given talents to the work in the prison. God softens the heart of the jail's warden so that Joseph is assigned responsibility over the other prisoners. Just as Potiphar was so confident in Joseph and his work, the warden now takes the same attitude. Joseph, though accused of attempted rape, is viewed as completely trustworthy by the prison officials. The Lord is not only sanctifying the heart and life of Joseph, He is prospering Joseph's work in such a way that many others around him notice it.

The thoughtful Christian who reads this story should not respond by saying, "O St. Joseph, pray for us!"

That would keep our attention upon man. The good news that the text keeps before us is that our faithful God the Lord is with Joseph. God is working, even in Egypt, even in events that are sordid, unseemly, and quite unfair.
The praise and glory goes to that covenant-keeping God. He has great things in store for Joseph, his family, indeed for the coming of the Kingdom of His Son, the Lord Jesus Christ, through this family.

Points to Ponder and Discuss

1. Daniel and his three friends are taken away as captives to Babylon (see Daniel 1). What are the similarities (as well as differences) between Joseph's situation and that of Daniel and his three friends?
2. When people are in positions of authority, they have power that belongs to that position or office. What are the dangers of having such power? That is to say, how can power be abused? How are people without power in danger of being abused and mistreated?
3. Is the emphasis in this chapter on what the Lord is doing, or is the emphasis on Joseph's courage and moral strength? Is Joseph being held up in the text as a "good example"? Why or why not?
4. Read 1 Corinthians 6:12–20. Check a Bible encyclopedia about what the city of Corinth was like morally. Have things changed much today? Paul says, "Flee from sexual immorality." Joseph had to flee physically from Potiphar's wife. Our bodies and our sexuality are wonderful gifts from God, but how has our society distorted those gifts? Where are the temptations to immorality today, also in our homes and communities?

5. To an unbeliever who reads Joseph's story, he appears to be a victim of "bad luck." But Christians know something much better and quite different about this story. Trace how the hand of God has kept guiding the destiny of Joseph, so that in peril of being killed, he instead is preserved and even promoted.

6. Read Psalm 1. This wisdom psalm describes the truly blessed man. It notes the two ways of life that a person can follow and the outcomes for each way (Ps. 1:6). How did Jesus Christ fulfill what this truly blessed Man is? How can this be seen in Joseph in Genesis 39?

Lesson 6

Joseph Interprets Two Dreams in Prison

Read Genesis 40

Introduction

Joseph escaped death from his brothers when in the pit earlier, and he has escaped death with the false accusation of Potiphar's wife. God's presence has certainly blessed him, and not just with barely escaping death. He had positively prospered in Potiphar's house, and he prospers again in prison. But we could well imagine that this young man wonders what God's wisdom and plan in all these events might be. If God is with him, then the route God has chosen has been a real roller-coaster!

New Prisoners Placed with Joseph (40:1–5)

This prison was not the worst place to stay. It was for criminals of "upper society," so to speak. What are called the "cupbearer" and "baker" in verse 1 are later called the "chief cupbearer" (verse 9) and "chief baker" (verse 16). When I was growing up and heard this story, the first character was called the (chief) "butler," a word that made me think of an older gentleman who wore a dark coat (with tails), who answered the door, and who spoke with an English accent! In fact, what older translations called the "butler" was, in fact, the cupbearer of the king. This was a very important position. Cupbearer had the responsibility of serving wine or beer to the Pharaoh, ensuring that it was

41

not only safe to drink, but that it was of the highest quality. Cupbearer in the ancient world often became confidants of the ruler, and if the cupbearer was wise and trustworthy, he frequently provided advice to the monarch.

Bakers were also important officials for the Egyptian rulers. It is likely that he oversaw the preparation of food for the Pharaoh on a daily basis. We must remember that the Egyptians believed that the Pharaoh was a living god, and therefore, he must receive the best and healthiest of foods. Bread was an important element in the Egyptian diet, a staple that was a central part of what Egyptians from all social classes would eat. In some written records from ancient Egypt, there are references to over twenty different kinds of breads and baked goods that Egyptians ate, including pastries and cakes.

Both of these important royal officials offended the Pharaoh in some way, but the text does not tell us what their offenses were. Did he get food poisoning? Bad wine? Burnt toast? Or, was the Pharaoh suspicious of something much more sinister? We do not know. The text keeps us focused on the important matters. Being imprisoned in the royal prison suggests that this was an incarceration to allow the Pharaoh to decide what to do with each man. The prison is only holding them for the time being.

Each man had a dream (verse 5). Scholars who have studied ancient Egyptian culture and religion tell us that the Egyptians believed that dreams were messages from the gods to tell the dreamer about future events. The ancient gods used dreams as a medium of revelation about what was soon to happen. But without interpretation, the cupbearer and the baker were discouraged.

The Cupbearer's Dream (40:6–15)

Dreams had proved to be troublesome for Joseph earlier in his life (see Gen. 37). Dreams, in fact, are important in

the entire Joseph story. They will typically come in pairs
as well. Two dreams in Genesis 37 revealed that Joseph
would rule over others, including his own family.
Two dreams in Genesis 40 reveal events concerned with
"lifting the head" in three days. And Pharaoh will have two
dreams later about seven cows and seven heads of grain.
God brings double dreams in these stories in order to
confirm His revelation to those who are receiving it,
whether such people are His own (like Joseph) or whether
they are pagans. God speaks to people where they are.
And "two or three witnesses" confirm that the message is true.

Joseph notices that the two important prisoners have
discouraged looks. When they confess to having had
dreams, but lack interpreters, Joseph makes a very
important statement in verse 8b: "Do not interpretations
belong to God? Tell me your dreams." In other words,
interpretations do not come from your pagan magicians or
superstitious priests. True revelation comes from God and
God alone! And Joseph sets himself up as being the
interpretive "point of contact" between the cupbearer's and
baker's dreams, on the one hand, and God Himself, on the
other hand. Joseph will receive God's explanation of the
dreams, and he will then relay that message. Here in the
prison, Joseph is a kind of "prophet" of God.

The first dream uses garden imagery: a vine with three
branches produces grapes. The cupbearer in the dream takes
these grapes, presses the juice into Pharaoh's cup, and offers
the cup to the Egyptian king.

Joseph knows its meaning: in three days, the cupbearer
will be restored to his important position in Pharaoh's court.
Good news for the cupbearer: release from prison in
three days! But Joseph is not done talking. He includes a
protestation of his innocence. He recalls his earlier
kidnapping ("forcibly carried off") and his more recent
arrest on false charges. He once was in a "pit" before being

sold as a slave, and now he is in a "pit" again! Prison is no picnic; it is a "hole." He knows that the facts are on his side, and he hopes that the cupbearer will take his case to the "supreme court" of Egypt, to Pharaoh himself.

The Chief Baker's Dream (40:16–19)

The baker is encouraged by Joseph's explanation of the cupbearer's dream. But he will not hear a good explanation. Three baskets on his head represent three days as well. But the bakery items and delicious pastries in the top basket are food for the birds. While the cupbearer's "head was lifted" (i.e., restored to office), the baker's "head will be lifted" as well, but in a different way. The baker will be hanged on a tree, and his body will be eaten by the birds. For an Egyptian, whose burial practices included mummification (at least for important people), such an end to his life would be utterly disgraceful.

Dreams Fulfilled, but Joseph Forgotten (40:20–23)

The third day comes, a birthday celebration for Pharaoh. It proves to be a restoration day for the chief cupbearer, but it is a day of devastation for the chief baker. Both men have their heads "lifted up" but in decidedly different fashions. The cupbearer resumes his service to the Egyptian monarch, while the baker is executed by hanging (or by impaling his body on a sharp pole).

Joseph may have entertained the hope that the cupbearer would take his story to the proper person, and he might soon be released from prison. But the days dragged on. Likely he would have realized in a few weeks that his situation was not going to change soon. Here is a test of faith, a trial of his personal confidence in God and His providential care. We recognize that the text of Genesis 40 does not reveal to us Joseph's inner thoughts, but it would be a long two years of prison (see Gen. 41:1). How is it possible for a man to forget the young slave in prison who so accurately interpreted his dream? Was it a matter of racial or social snobbery, that is, royal officials really don't care for slaves placed in prison? We are not told. But the words are a sad conclusion to the chapter: "The chief cupbearer...forgot him." It is as if he thinks, "I got my break; too bad for you, Joseph."

Two dreams...again! Joseph had caught the drift of meaning in the dreams he had when he was 17 years old (Gen. 37), and he will later interpret the two dreams of Pharaoh in Genesis 41. The story of dreams in the royal dungeon is part of a pattern that links us to the other dream stories. The first set of dreams got the young man in trouble with his brothers. The dreams of this chapter speak of life and death, but his interpretation would be forgotten until later. The dreams of Pharaoh would convince the Egyptian ruler that Joseph was the man in touch with God Himself, when he correctly interprets them. In this way, Joseph is a kind of prophet, someone with true knowledge of God and His plans for the future.

God Still Moves in a Mysterious Way

Joseph again has shown to people around him—and to us readers—that his confidence in God is met with God granting to him understanding of dreams, the ability to interpret them correctly. There is nothing magical in Joseph's soul: it is God who gives interpretations to those He chooses. This is still true today: where God has deposited a record of His will, a written testimony of His heart and mind, we do well to listen and obey. That is found in His Word, the Bible, an inspired text that is necessary, clear, sufficient, and fully authoritative. Those who drink in its message are modern day "prophets" who have the mind of Christ, able to address the questions of our day and age with the will of God.

In Genesis 40, the stage is set for the great developments of Genesis 41. Chapter 40 is pivotal for the career of Joseph in Egypt and for the coming of the Kingdom of God. Even in prison he is successful. Surely God is with him so that he continues to rise toward the top. Consider the following: he is not murdered; he is sold to Potiphar; he is not executed but only imprisoned. Truly God is with him. That fact does not spare him from occasional harsh treatment or temptation. "The bud may have a bitter taste, but sweet will be the flower." Could Joseph see that truth? Can our faith grasp such things still today?

Points to Ponder and Discuss

1. God spoke to the covenant people before the coming of Christ in a variety of ways (Heb. 1:1, 2). Besides dreams, what are some of the other ways that God spoke to His people in Old Testament times? Does He sometimes speak in these ways today?

2. In Jeremiah 23:25–32 the Lord denounces the false prophets who preach their own dreams and prophesy lies. A true prophet should stand in God's council, because then he hears and knows the true revelation of God (see Jer. 23:16–18, 21–22). How can Christians today know that the preaching they hear is truly God's Word (see 1 John 4:1–6)?

3. By explaining the two dreams, Joseph is showing the light of God's Word to these Egyptians. What can we say about Joseph gaining confidence in a role of bearing the light to Egypt, for Israel (later)?

4. Joseph is innocent, a victim of injustice, first from his brothers and then from Potiphar's wife. How did our Lord respond when He was falsely accused before the Sanhedrin? How should Christians respond today when they become the objects of false accusations, trumped-up charges? How did Paul and Silas respond in Acts 16 when they were arrested? (Note what they say on the morning after the earthquake when the authorities want to release them.)

5. This chapter marks the low point in Joseph's life: he is imprisoned. Release comes in the next chapter. Describe how Joseph responds to his situation, both in Potiphar's household and now in prison. Do we ever sense any bitterness in Joseph? His diligence and attention to responsibility is "rewarded" in both situations in what ways? Do believers always see similar results? Is there a kind of Biblical principle at play here? See Luke 16:10–12.

6. What place do honesty and hard work have in the Kingdom of God? Are not unbelievers also honest and hard-working at times? How can we make a greater impact for the coming of God's Kingdom by how we act, speak, and work in the places of our occupations?

Joseph Interprets Pharaoh's Dreams

Read Genesis 40:1–36

Introduction

Joseph had received revelation and understanding from God for the dreams of the chief cupbearer and the chief butler. Joseph wants out of prison, and he asks the cupbearer to take his appeal to Pharaoh himself. But nothing happens for two full years. God is with Joseph, it is true, but Joseph must learn patience through what he suffers. Dreams have brought Joseph trouble, but they also provided a means to impress two royal officials in prison about Joseph's abilities. More dreams are on the way in this chapter. At one level, the dreams of Pharaoh, the ruler over Egypt, will confirm the dreams that Joseph had when he was 17 years old. By interpreting Pharaoh's dreams, Joseph will show that he can rule and have authority in Egypt, for "the Spirit of God" is with him. The prophetic dreams of Genesis 37 are about to be fulfilled.

Impossible Dreams of Cows and Grain (41:1–8)

We know that the Pharaoh was only a man, merely a particular human being who ruled ancient Egypt. But the Egyptians viewed him much differently. The ancient Egyptian religion and worldview held that Pharaoh had a very special relationship to all the other gods and goddesses. In fact, they believed that Pharaoh was a living god, the deity

Horus incarnate, and that Pharaoh was the figure who held the nation together and provided it with order. As the French king Louis XIV would later boast, "I am the state," so too the Pharaoh was the heart of the Egyptian state, it was believed. For him to have a troubling dream would have disturbed all in his court. Added to this was their belief that dreams must have some meaning, and if the meaning of any dream is unknown, this could develop into a small-time crisis for the Egyptian monarch.

But Pharaoh is only a man, a human who has dreams as we all do. In one night he has two dreams. The first dream has seven healthy cows coming out of the Nile River. Cows in Egypt would often graze in the reed grasses by the river, sometimes going partially into the water to cool off and escape pesky insects. This Pharaoh sees. But then, something disturbing occurs in the dream: seven ugly and thin cows come up after the others, and they devour the good cows. As anyone of us can attest, when a troubling or violent thing happens in our dreams, we may be jolted awake. Pharaoh wakes up.

But the night is not over. He dozes off into sleep, only to have a second dream with many elements parallel to the first dream. This time it is not fat and thin cows; instead it is seven plump and seven blighted heads of grain. And again, as in the first dream, the thin, blighted heads of grain devour the seven good heads of grain. Pharaoh is again startled awake, only to realize that he has had another disturbing dream. We generally forget our dreams (at least I do!); they somehow rarely write themselves onto our memory "hard drive." But Pharaoh remembers them quite well. They have troubled him.

Pharaoh, thought to be a living "god," cannot explain his own dreams. He has magicians and wise men as religious experts in his court. He tells them his two dreams, and his religious experts with all their wisdom and cleverness are not able to interpret the dreams either. The entire Egyptian court is still in the dark; their achievements in religious studies and Egyptian theology have provided them with no help to solve the riddle of dreams about cannibal cows and thin heads of grain that eat other heads of grain. Ph.D.'s in "dreamology" are not going to provide any answers this time around. All the wise men and magicians are stumped!

Now the Cupbearer Remembers Joseph (41:9–13)

This pathetic little "crisis" over two dreams now jolts the cupbearer's memory, and he steps forward to confess his shortcomings (literally, "my sins"), namely, he had met Joseph two years earlier, a Hebrew slave who actually explained his own dream in a most accurate way. But after he had been released the cupbearer had said nothing about Joseph! In describing Joseph to Pharaoh the cupbearer does not even name him (did he completely forget his name? Did he so disdain this "young Hebrew" that he could not even be bothered with his name?). Since we readers are "all-knowing" (in a literary sense), we already know from Genesis 40 that the Lord is with Joseph and that He provides him with the proper interpretation. Pharaoh is about to learn who Joseph is; we readers already know him.

Joseph: From Internment to Interpreter (41:14–36)

Pharaoh, eager to know what his dreams mean, orders Joseph to be brought before him. However, before Joseph could ever hope to come before a "living god," he must be properly prepared. Things move fast now as Joseph is quickly brought (literally, "made to run") from the pit. His body and head are shaved (the Egyptians were a bit fanatical about cleanliness), and a fresh change of clothes is given to him. Psalm 105:20 says, "The king sent and released him, the ruler of peoples set him free."

Pharaoh tells this young man, just fresh out of the royal dungeon, that he has heard that Joseph is able to interpret dreams. Joseph's response is quite striking: "Not I! It is God who will give Pharaoh the answer that explains what his dream means." Whatever else Joseph has learned in prison, he continues to remember and believe that he is a child of God, that God has all the answers, and that God must be given the full credit that He deserves. One might say that Joseph embraces the life motto, "*Soli Deo Gloria*—to God be the glory alone!" Joseph could have said, "Yes, I have insight into dreams." But he stays true to his earlier confession, when he had said to the chief cupbearer and the chief baker that interpretations belong to God (see Gen. 40:8).

Pharaoh relates his dreams to Joseph, and he does so with some embellishment. Probably the most notable item that is added is that after the lean, ugly cows devour the fat cows, the lean cows are just as lean and ugly as before. In other words, once the lean years are past, Egypt's resources will be largely spent.

Joseph then interprets. Now, we must remember that a (royal) prophet must be accurate: Joseph would have forfeited his life had he been wrong. The dreams are in fact "the same" (41:25, 26). The fact that there were two dreams is significant (41:32): God has confirmed the message with "two witnesses" in order to help establish the truth being communicated in the dreams (as He had done in Joseph's dreams in Genesis 37). All of this discredits the magicians and wise men of Egypt: it is not that they have a "wrong" interpretation of Pharaoh's dreams; they have no answer at all. They are completely clueless! God's ways have put to shame the wisdom of this world, just as God's grace may appear to be foolishness to the world. In fact it is wiser and more powerful than anything this present evil age has to offer (cf. 1 Cor. 1:18ff.).

But Joseph is not finished speaking. In a rather bold move, he goes on to tell Pharaoh what course of action he should take. First, appoint a wise man to be in charge of Egypt. Second, Pharaoh should appoint commissioners to take a fifth of all harvests during the years of plenty and store all this food in the various cities of Egypt. Joseph has in mind the well-being of the country. A wise ruler knows that a hungry citizenry can easily turn into an angry, even revolutionary, mob. Remember the cry of the mobs during the Bolshevik revolution in Russia was, "Peace, land, and bread!" Joseph is thinking about the well-being of the Egyptian people, for in their well-being the Pharaoh could experience stability in his reign.

Joseph in Egypt, Daniel in Babylon

Many Bible readers have seen parallels in what happens to Joseph here and what happens to Daniel later during the Exile in Babylon. Both men are taken in their youth against their wills to foreign lands, there to be exploited by pagans. Joseph is sold as a slave, and Daniel (with his three friends) would be groomed to become a "new man" in Babylon (new name, royal diet, Babylonian education and worldview, etc.). Satan would try his best to crush these young men so that they would not be effective in God's work. But God was with these godly young men so that in showing obedience and loyalty to this same God, God prospers them in very deliberate and noticeable ways.

Allen Ross (*Creation and Blessing*, p. 637) identifies four similarities between Joseph and Daniel:

1. Both men are Hebrew slaves who are summoned before the king to interpret his dream.
2. The king explains that problem of the dream that has eluded the wise men of his court.
3. With God's help, each man interprets the dream of the king.
4. The foreign king elevates the Hebrew in reward for resolving the problem of his dream.

With both Joseph and Daniel, the so-called wisdom of
the court magicians and wise men is seen to be foolish
and ineffective. God clearly comes out as all-wise and
decidedly on the side of His own people, even if they are
held captive in a foreign land. God's hand is not shortened;
His Word is never bound.
The Pharaoh is being confronted with the Word of God
in the mouth of a man of God (Nebuchadnezzar will receive
the same, centuries later). Pharaoh might not acknowledge it
in the right way. Joseph is virtually the equivalent of the
Word of God in the role he plays (see S. de Graaf, *Promise
and Deliverance*, I:229). Joseph's promotion paves the way
for Israel's "redemption" by a 400+ year sojourn in the land
of Egypt. Egypt is not yet an object for conversion or evangelism,
but that great day would come later through Christ.

Points to Ponder and Discuss
1. Joseph underwent several trials in his life, including his
   younger years. He was hated by his brothers (nearly
   killed), sold as a slave, falsely accused by Potiphar's wife
   and then imprisoned. What are some things that he
   might have learned in all these trials?
2. God does not give us special revelation via dreams in this
   redemptive era. How do we gain understanding today in
   the issues that confront human beings, communities,
   and nations?
3. James 1:2 tells us to "consider it pure joy...whenever
   you face trials of many kinds." How can we do that?
   Do we rejoice in the suffering, *or*, does Scripture tell us
   to focus on what the Lord is teaching us in the suffering?
   What are some of the things that James 1:2–4 says Christians
   may develop in the midst of suffering? How can a
   believer gain wisdom during his or her sufferings?

4. Read Matthew 2:1–12. King Herod would also be confronted by a revelation from heaven, a star that appears to wise men from the East. Jewish religious leaders will point to the prophecy of Micah to provide some kind of explanation and interpretation. In the dreams to Pharaoh, in the star from the East, and in the Biblical prophecy of Micah, powerful rulers are confronted with the Word of God. How do they respond to that Word? How are their responses different? What are the consequences to their responses?

5. Read 1 Corinthians 1:18–31. How does God make foolish the "wisdom" of Egypt by giving Joseph the interpretation of Pharaoh's dreams? How has God supremely made Jewish desire for signs and Greek interest in wisdom look weak and foolish? Does God need the wise, influential, and powerful people in His program? What use does God make of the "foolishness of preaching" (*not*, foolish preaching!)? Where is our true Christian boasting now?

6. Do Christians have a responsibility to address rulers today with God's Word? Why or why not?

Joseph Cares for Egypt... and the World

Read Genesis 41:37–57

Introduction

The transition for Joseph in one day is breath-taking.
One moment he is still in the royal dungeon of Egypt, and
then next moment he is being rushed to get cleaned up and
properly clothed in order to stand before Pharaoh.
God's timing is not always personally comfortable, but His
timing is the best, never too early or too late. God sent the
dreams that disturbed the Egyptian king, and God used the
occasion to awaken the chief cupbearer's memory
concerning a "Hebrew lad" who perfectly interpreted two
dreams two years earlier. The spotlight now falls upon
Joseph again so that he can be the agent of revelation to the
royal pagan court.

Pharaoh is Impressed! (41:37–44)

   Joseph not only has provided an accurate interpretation of
Pharaoh's dreams, but Joseph also gives Pharaoh unsolicited
advice about how to guide the nation through the next
several years. This defies sense! Who would have thought
that a foreigner ("Hebrew"), a youth, someone from the
dungeon, serving a sentence for assaulting the wife of a
high Egyptian official—who would think that such a
person would now be telling a "living god" how to run
his country? God's ways are certainly not our ways, but

they are amazing to behold! Pharaoh did not have the interpretation to his own dreams, and his magicians and "wise" men did not know what the solution was, but God gave all answers to Joseph. And these pagans recognize that Joseph has spoken with true wisdom.

Pharaoh is led to confess that the "spirit of God" is found in no one else but in Joseph. Pharaoh's advisers are reduced to silence; they are now "dumb" in more ways than one. To Pharaoh, Joseph has the "spirit of God," not in the sense of Holy Spirit, since the Pharaoh is not a Trinitarian. Still, to the New Testament believer, Pharaoh's words resonate on that level: Christian believers know that the Holy Spirit of God is with Joseph to give him understanding of both dreams and insight into a national crisis that will be present in seven years time.

Pharaoh promotes Joseph, putting on him the royal signet ring, fine linen robes (new clothes again!), and a gold chain. He gets his own limousine (actually, a chariot), which Egyptians are obliged to greet with acts of bowing and homage. Pharaoh remains the head of the state, but in fact Joseph is in charge. "Without your word no one will lift hand or foot in all Egypt," Pharaoh tells Joseph (verse 44).

Joseph Acquires a Family (41:45, 50–52)

Pharaoh is not finished with Joseph. He also renames him with the name Zaphenath-Paneah. While we may not be certain as to the exact meaning of this name, John Currid (*Genesis*, vol. 2, p. 271) suggests that it means "God speaks and he lives." This probably is to make this young Hebrew more presentable as an Egyptian to the rest of the country. In addition, Pharaoh gives Joseph a wife, Asenath ("she belongs to [goddess] Neith"), a woman taken from the upper ranks of Egyptian society (her father is an Egyptian priest!). Asenath comes from a priestly family in the city of On, where a temple to the sun god, Re, existed.

She probably would not have been Joseph's choice as a wife, and we can only wonder what religious influence he would have on his Egyptian wife. From all that the Bible reveals to us about Joseph, it seems assured that he maintained his faith in the one true God, and doubtless, he testified to Asenath about this true God. Furthermore, since Asenath is the only wife mentioned, we may assume (although we cannot prove it) that Joseph was monogamous (in contrast to his father Jacob).

Within the seven years of bumper crops, Joseph also experiences a good "harvest" in his own marriage. Two sons are born to him and Asenath. Children are truly a heritage of the Lord! The firstborn son is named "Manasseh," a name which sounds like the verb "forget." He says on the occasion of Manasseh's birth and naming, "It is because God has made me forget all my trouble and all my father's household." This son helps Joseph erase some of the pain that he had experienced in Jacob's family. The second son is named "Ephraim," meaning something like "double fruitfulness." He exclaims, "It is because God has made me fruitful (again!) in the land of my suffering." Certainly we feel Joseph's joy in the birth of two sons. From this point on in the Biblical record, Joseph will not experience any more dramatic setbacks, at least nothing on the order of the earlier imprisonments that he had suffered from Israelite or Egyptian alike. He will remain an important official in Egypt until the day he dies, many decades later.

Joseph Acquires Plenty of Food (41:46–49)

Joseph is 30 years old (verse 46) when he is promoted to being vizier, the second in charge of all Egypt, something like a modern-day prime minister. In thirteen years he has gone from being a boy hated by his own brothers, to becoming the functional ruler (under Pharaoh) of the entire land of Egypt! It is not that Joseph is personally clever in escaping trouble: the Lord God was with him, enabling him to escape and to use his God-given talents and wisdom with very powerful effects.

Joseph steps up to the plate as he is assigned a great task, namely, securing the food of Egypt in anticipation of a great period of famine. He travels throughout the entire land of Egypt, becoming familiar with the land, its agriculture, its officials, and its people. He has been assigned high honor, but it does not go to his head in order to inflate his ego.

The seven years of plenty begin. Normally, the seasonal flooding of the Nile River sets up the situations that lead to good years of food production. The flooding deposits rich soil along the Nile banks, enabling fields to produce bumper crops. What was different now during the seven years of plenty, we cannot be sure. In any case, the food coming in during harvest seasons is overwhelming, "like the sand of the sea," the same kind of language that God had used to describe the number of children to be given to Abraham and Jacob (see Gen. 22:17 and 32:12). Food harvested near particular cities was stored in those cities. Joseph now gathers the food "beyond measure" (verse 49), so much, in fact, that record-keeping breaks down. But God, who controls the seasons and all harvests, was providing so much grain in these seven years because it would have to be enough to carry Egypt (and many others!) through a seven year period of famine.

In addition, in a world in which public officials are corrupted by money and prestige, using high office to line their own pockets, we may well believe that Joseph did his honest best to make suitable arrangements to store food supplies throughout Egypt. Had he not done his job well, when the famine came to strike the land, there would not have been enough food, and then Joseph would have lost his life. Even in a totalitarian state like ancient Egypt, rulers (like Joseph) are

servants of the Most High God, ones who must someday give
to God an account of their office (see Romans 13:1ff.).

Joseph Feeds the World (41:53–57)

The period of famine comes, "just as Joseph had said"
(verse 54). This famine is not limited to Egypt, but people
are getting hungry everywhere. People cried out for food,
but Pharaoh directed people to Joseph. The "living god"
can do nothing, but the man of God is in charge.
Furthermore, the sense of the wording in verses 56–57 is
that Joseph wisely rationed out food to Egyptians and to
others who came to Egypt for food. In this way, something
of the words of Genesis 12:1–3 are coming true here.
God had promised that through the seed of Abram, all the
nations of the world will be blessed. A great-grandson of
Abram, a young man named Joseph, is bringing physical
blessings to many people in his day. This is a sketch, an
outline, of what a later Son of Abraham, Jesus Christ,
would do in bringing life, abundant life, to all the nations
of the world.

Joseph experienced both humiliation and exaltation.
By God's grace alone, he remained faithful to God, who has
a great plan that He works out through all the twists and
turns of our lives. Our calling is to be faithful to this God
and the work that He assigns to us. Joseph becomes
responsible for feeding Egypt and later the rest of "the
world" (at least, the eastern end of the Mediterranean).
God placed Joseph here for the sake of the Lord Jesus
Christ and the rescue of God's people. Indeed, in so many
ways Joseph's life and career anticipate and parallel so
much in Christ's own life. His own would not receive him,
he is lowered into the pit (like a grave), then raised to rule
at the right hand of the authority, in charge of all things so
that blessings might be distributed to many. No, Joseph is
not Jesus Christ, but God is drawing out a pattern here that

we will see fleshed out in fullness and in reality when Jesus Christ comes into this world. For our heavenly Father has given all authority to our risen Lord Jesus Christ (see Matt. 28:18) so that everyone in need might go to Him, and He will tell us what to do (see Gen. 41:55; Matt. 28:18–20).

Points to Ponder and Discuss

1. We love to hear about "rags to riches" stories, about how a person in less than favorable circumstances is able to overcome the odds and rise to success. How is the story of Joseph's appointment as overseer of Egypt *not* just another "rags to riches" story? Does Joseph "succeed" through blind fate or his own cleverness?

2. Joseph not only receives insight from the Lord in order to interpret the dreams, but he also sees what needs to be done for the whole nation. Once appointed second-in-command of Egypt, he gets to work. In this sense, one might call Joseph an "entrepreneur." Wisdom, coupled with hard work, also belongs to the Christian calling. How can Christians apply Biblical insights and concrete efforts in the area of education today, or business, or politics? How do we pool our resources together for these efforts?

3. Read Psalm 104. What does the Bible teach us about God's providence? See Heidelberg Catechism, Lord's Day 10, and Westminster Confession of Faith, chapter V. How do people today respond to prosperity or to disasters? How do Christians respond to these things, and how should they respond?

4. Through Joseph's efforts, there was food available for the hungry of Egypt and neighboring countries. Does this story teach us that the government is responsible for feeding the hungry when all else fails? Why or why not? What role do God's people have in taking care of the poor and hungry?

5. We know that Daniel later will arouse jealousy and hatred from other royal officials (see Daniel 6). Let's speculate just a little. What do you think may have been the attitude of the Egyptian magicians and "wise men" toward the promotion of this Hebrew young man to second in charge in all Egypt? Were they perhaps afraid of him, jealous of him, in awe of him? If Potiphar and his wife are still living, what must they think? (Remember, we are only speculating...)

6. Joseph shows that he can stay focused on his task, his calling. In Potiphar's house, he is a good and faithful servant, in the prison Joseph is the same, a good and faithful servant. He receives promotion, even though he goes through periods of trouble. Faithfulness results in promotion. Is this something of a fluke, a quirk in God's providence, or is a general biblical principle seen to be at work here? Read Luke 16:10–16: "He who is faithful in little, is faithful also in much." What do Christians learn here?

Joseph Puts His Brothers on Trial

Read Genesis 42:1–28

Introduction

The famine strikes Egypt just as the dreams had indicated and just as Joseph had said. God had sent the dreams, gave Joseph the interpretation, and sent the famine, thus confirming Joseph in his role as a kind of prophet in Egypt. God had raised him from the pit of prison to the pinnacle of power and privilege. Joseph is a young man in his thirties, and Pharaoh tells anyone who is hungry, "Go to Joseph and do what he tells you" (Gen. 41:55). Egypt has food, and Joseph controls access to its supply. This now becomes important for the unfolding of God's redemptive plan, because the famine has also reached into Canaan, and it impacts the family of Jacob as well. This suggests that the famine is caused not only by poor flooding by the Nile, but also by insufficient rainfall in Canaan. So, the crisis spreads. It will be a crisis over food that will serve to bring the family of Jacob back into the life of Joseph, although his identity will remain hidden from them for some time.

This chapter can be divided along geographic lines: in Canaan (verses 1–5), then in Egypt (verses 6–28), and then back in Canaan again (verses 29–38). This lesson will focus on the scene in Canaan and then the events in Egypt. The next lesson will deal with the brothers back with father Jacob in Canaan.

Standing in the Bread Line (42:1–5)

Travel and trade between Egypt and Canaan were not unusual activities, and therefore we are not surprised to read that news reaches Canaan that Egypt is surviving the current famine rather well. Egypt becomes again the "bread basket" for the eastern Mediterranean region. When Jacob hears that food is available in Egypt, he addresses his sons basically by saying, "Why are you sitting around just staring at each other? Get up and go buy food for us!" Apparently even the food resources of Jacob and all his children have fallen on hard times so that their pantries and food stocks are running low.

In sending his sons to Egypt, Jacob very deliberately keeps Benjamin from going along with them. It is not because Benjamin is too young: he is over twenty years old. He is afraid "that harm might come to him" (verse 4). It is somewhat unclear whether Jacob's fears are concerned with some unfortunate incident that may happen to Benjamin while in Egypt, by Egyptians, or whether he harbors some fears about something happening to Benjamin from his ten sons. To father Jacob, Benjamin is not merely the youngest son, he is the only surviving son of Rachel, his beloved wife, and thus a replacement for Joseph. Shortly after Benjamin had been born, Rachel died. The last time Jacob had seen Joseph, that favorite son, he had left home with his special coat on a journey to find his brothers and their herds. Jacob is shown that very same coat, now smeared with blood, and he had concluded that "a wild animal" had devoured his son. But the reader wonders whether Jacob thinks that perhaps his ten sons know more about Joseph's disappearance than what they let on. In any case, to be sure that Benjamin remains alive, Jacob keeps him home.

Hunger has reduced the family of Jacob (referred to as Israel in verse 5) to people who are no better than any other hungry folks. The covenant sons will have to go to the same "grocery store" called Egypt like everyone else, and they will have to stand in line to buy their share. This famine has not discriminated between the pagans and the family of God. But God has His saving purposes at work in all this.

Joseph Arrests His Brothers as a Test (42:6–17)

Verse 6 summarizes what we had read earlier in Genesis 41:54–57. Joseph is revealed as a true *prophet* (41:54), as a *potentate* (a great ruler; 41:55), and an able *provider* (41:56). The result in verse 57 is that "all the earth" comes *to Joseph* for food. He clearly images what the Christ is today par excellence. Consider what this meant: Joseph now controls, directly or indirectly, the political and economic well-being of many peoples. And that will involve his family as well, although they will not know that for some time.

In reading narrative, the reader is always "all-knowing," literarily speaking. But Joseph is also almost all-knowing, and this serves to heighten the dramatic tension in this story. He recognizes his brothers, but they do not recognize him. Of course not! They have assumed that he was dead (or, at best, slaving away in some house or field). Joseph remains hid from their eyes since he was dressed like an Egyptian, almost certainly clean-shaven (Semites were typically bearded), and he uses a translator to communicate with them.

We should not miss how the text arranges the details of the first visit. After reminding us in verse 6 that Joseph is the governor of the land as well as the distributor of food, then we are told that the ten brothers bow down to him as ruler and provider. Joseph recognizes them, but he pretends to be a stranger to them. In his recognition of them, coupled with their bowing down to the ground before him, he now recalls his dreams from years earlier. Some things are now coming together, but Joseph does not let on all that he knows. Although Egyptian policy allowed people to cross the borders to engage in trade, Joseph seeks to turn on them by accusing them of being spies. He is humbling them and testing what kind of men his brothers are.

But is this really a test? Is it not rather punishment? After all, these ten brothers are the very men who had first plotted to kill Joseph, only holding back because he was blood relation, but then selling him in order to make a profit from his disappearance. In effect, that sale to traveling merchants was the equivalent to murder in that Joseph was now out of their life, once and for all (or so they thought). Murder is any desire that seeks to remove that neighbor whom God has placed next to you. And actions follow desires. This is the sin of the ten brothers, and they have never been held to account for their actions. As they stand before Joseph, he is in a position to administer justice to them. Did they not deserve judgment?

Joseph Tests His Brothers in a Second Way (42:18–28)

The ten brothers interpret these harsh circumstances as judgment for their cruel treatment of Joseph earlier. In verse 21 they literally say, "We are truly guilty." Joseph's pleas with them when he was in the pit (Gen. 37) and Jacob's tearful grief have not moved them as these events have. Reuben (verse 22) states that Joseph's blood is now demanded or required of them. The events of years before continue to trouble Reuben and apparently his brothers with him. Here is where we remember that it was Reuben, the oldest son of Jacob, who had planned to rescue Joseph from the pit and then send him back home. But Joseph was sold before Reuben's rescue could be carried out. It seems that Reuben's conscience has been vexed for all these years.

Reuben's statement is an echo of Genesis 9:5, which says, "And for your lifeblood I will surely demand an accounting...from each man, too, I will demand an accounting for the life of his fellow man." Sometimes we hear it said, "What goes around, comes around," as if the world is governed by some kind of impersonal principle of (Hindu or new age) karma, that notion of rewards and punishments that govern what happens to people. Or you may say, "He got what was coming to him."

But the world is not governed by impersonal forces. Our lives are not determined by mechanistic abstractions. This world is a moral universe, governed by a powerful, wise, and just God.

Joseph singles out Simeon for imprisonment. A likely reason may be that he has understood Reuben's words to his brothers as a kind of exoneration of Reuben. Reuben did not want the boy to be harmed, but Reuben was not present when the brothers sold him to the traveling merchants. If age was a factor in terms of "who is in charge," then Simeon as the second oldest would likely have been "in charge" while Reuben was gone. Joseph knows then exactly which of his brothers he will imprison. While we cannot prove that this is the reason, it is a plausible explanation. Simeon apparently had done nothing to stop the sale of Joseph into slavery. The brothers now watch as Simeon is arrested, bound, and taken away to prison. They are completely helpless to stop it.

But the picture is not completely bleak. They are given grain and provisions for the journey. They do not know that the money is waiting for its discovery in each man's grain bag. On the journey back, one of them opens his grain sack and discovers that his money is there. They have escaped imprisonment in Egypt, but this new discovery does not fill them with joy. Rather, they are filled with dread. In the text of the Bible, this is the first recorded instance of the brothers referring to God (see verse 28). They interpret this event not as a chance mistake by the Egyptian officials, but as an event directed by God Himself. But their interpretation does not go any farther. They are not yet at the point where they would say something along the lines of the Apostle Paul, "God works all things for the good of those who love Him" (cf. Rom. 8:28). They are men with guilty consciences, and now events take on a more ominous meaning.

Jesus Christ is the ruler over all creation, and He is the discerner of all hearts and consciences. As a father disciplines the children he loves, so Christ also disciplines congregations and Christian believers. Can we see the Spirit of Christ working through this "harsh lord of the land," not for destruction, but for the kind of godly maturity that God seeks in all His children? Behind Joseph, is God our Father in Jesus Christ.

Points to Ponder and Discuss

1. Reflect on how much food is available in nearby grocery stores. "Give us this day our daily bread," we pray, but in our hearts we would rather have a nice steak and pie with ice cream. How easy is it to pray for "daily bread" when food supplies in North America are available in such great abundance? What would our society be like if all food production were to stop tomorrow?

2. How does the bowing of the ten brothers to Joseph remind him of his dreams in Genesis 37? Is Joseph beginning now to put the prophetic "pieces of the puzzle" together in regard to what God has in store for him as a ruler over even his family? In other words, how do the two dreams of Genesis 37 put light on what is happening in Genesis 42? If you read into the next several chapters, how much bowing is done by the several characters in this story?

3. The consciences of Joseph's brothers begin to speak in Genesis 42. Conscience is a God-given part of our own

hearts and minds, and it is wonderful when that conscience operates according to what God wants for us as beings created in His image. What does it mean when a person has a "seared conscience"? What happens when a person's conscience is sinfully twisted or even basically dead?

4. What kind of subtle message might Joseph be giving to his own brothers when he says in verse 18, "Do this and you will live, for I fear God." Perhaps the ten brothers think that the Egyptian ruler is afraid of his own (Egyptian) god. But could it have awakened in them thoughts about what the true God would expect from them?

5. Joseph's words and actions strike real fear into his brothers. Was this the right thing to do? Is it possible that there is a kind of perverse delight in Joseph's heart as he watches his brothers squirm just a bit? How does verse 24 fit into the picture of what is in Joseph's soul? If he really loves them, why does he not reveal himself to them, then and there, before they set off back to Canaan?

6. In what ways have you experienced God's discipline in your life?

Joseph's Test Continues in Jacob's Household

Read Genesis 42:29–38

Introduction

The first audience of the ten brothers with Joseph did not go smoothly at all. It almost certainly did not occur to them as they had entered Egypt that they would be singled out and accused of being spies, held in custody, with Simeon arrested before they are permitted to return to Canaan. The harsh treatment comes from this mighty ruler of Egypt who says that he is concerned for the security of the Egyptian homeland. It is nowhere in the mind of the brothers that this harsh ruler is their own younger brother Joseph, and he has recognized them very well. Their bowing before him reminds him of the dreams of several decades earlier. The rough treatment has awakened certain thoughts in their conscience, and their hearts are heavy as they return to their father Jacob.

Jacob's Sons Report to Their Father (42:29–34)

The Biblical text gives a rather lengthy description of what the ten brothers report to their father. It is important to listen to them speak, both in terms of what they say and what they do not say. They have no proper name of the Egyptian official who spoke so harshly with them. He is called "the man who is lord over the land" (verses 30 and 33).

There is one enormous gap in the brothers' report to Jacob. We do not hear any hint in their words of a pricked conscience. There is no hint that something from their past, hidden in the depths of their hearts but now resurfacing, should be reported. How wonderful it would sound if we read something like the following at the end of their travel report: "Father, there is something else that we have to tell you. Please sit down, for this is something that happened years ago, something very sad, and we have to confess to you a terrible thing that we did." But those words we do not hear. In Egypt, their consciences have been tested and awakened. They even talk about it with each other. But they cannot bring themselves to confess their dirty deeds to their father. Instead, they dutifully tell Jacob what they had said to the harsh Egyptian lord, "We are honest men..." (verse 31).

Some ironies stand out in all this. First, though they claim they are "honest," we know that they have not been wholly honest. They stand in Joseph's presence and declare that they were "twelve brothers, sons of one father" (verse 32). How true! Joseph—unrecognized by them— is also part of that group of "twelve." Also, in Genesis 37 they came home with money, that of their sale of Joseph. They will again come home with money, this time with their returned money in their grain sacks.

Sad Confusion in Jacob's Household (42:35–38)

After they have finished telling Jacob the story of their harrowing trip to buy grain, they all discover something in their grain bags, something that only one of them had found earlier on the return trip (verse 27). We read this part of the story before we hear the reaction of Jacob. The earlier discovery of the money had shaken them, but now they all— the ten brothers and their father—are frightened. We usually feel good when a store clerk gives us back too much change...just before we point that out and return the money we should not have (if we are "honest" people!). But the household of Jacob is further frightened by this discovery of money. They know that they had handed over the silver to buy the grain that they have taken back from Egypt. That part was clear. But now, how in the world had that same money returned to them in their sacks of grain? Surely the Egyptians were not so foolish as to put the money of every brother back in each grain bag. If this is truly an act of God, then what is God saying to them? Why did God do this? We might well conclude that the brothers and Jacob their father are all spooked by this.

Jacob's reaction is, first of all, not about his uneasiness over the returned money. For him, the crucial thing is the loss of his sons: Joseph is gone, Simeon is likely gone as well, and the loss of Benjamin now threatens. He blames his existing sons for all this: "You have deprived me of my children!" (verse 36). Is he implying somehow that the loss of Joseph should also be placed at their feet and accounted against them? "Everything is against me!" he cries out in anguish.

Reuben steps forward with a most clumsy offer. He had tried to protect Joseph earlier, almost certainly out of loving respect for his father. Now he offers to be the protector of Benjamin, holding out the prospect of his own sons as security. But how is this any comfort to Jacob? Says Reuben, "You can kill my sons if I fail to bring Benjamin back in safety." Most unlikely! Jacob would never be satisfied if, having lost Benjamin, that he then turns around to kill two grandsons. What is Reuben thinking?

We should not down-play the terror and fear that Jacob experiences here. He has already lost his favorite son, Joseph, and there is no promise that he will ever see Simeon again. On top of that, this harsh Egyptian lord is demanding to see his very youngest son Benjamin. Even more, Reuben offers to have his two sons executed if Benjamin does not return. Jacob's words come very close to an actual accusation against his sons when he says,

"If harm comes to him on the journey you are taking, you will bring my gray head down to the grave in sorrow." In effect, Jacob says that the proposed actions of his sons may well kill him. Jacob is at an advanced age, and we should not dismiss these words as overly melodramatic: his heart has been scarred, and it would not take much more for tragic events to hasten his death. The question about their guilt had actually come up earlier in a comment made by father Jacob when he cries out in verse 36, "You have deprived me of my children; Joseph is no more...you would take..." His cry is almost Job-like, but with this difference: Job does not know why all this has happened in terms of what he has lost.

The Mercy of the "Court"

The trouble Joseph gives his ten brothers highlights their guilt. Joseph is seeking honest men. That is what they had said they were. So now, they must prove or substantiate their claim. His tests are seeking to draw out where they are really at. But Joseph also shows them mercy. Consider these facts:

1. If he really thought they are spies, he would have killed them. What ruler in the ancient world would have given it a second thought about killing people that he thought were spies?
2. Only Simeon is imprisoned after the three-day imprisonment. Again, if they are all spies, put them all in prison. But Joseph singles out only one man. This should appear merciful to them.
3. He allows grain to go with them on their return. Okay, a somewhat tolerant ruler in the ancient world might let suspicious characters go free, but what ruler would still sell them any grain at all?
4. He returned their all their money. Joseph is not after their money. He wants to know their heart. The brothers

do not know that Joseph returned the money, but the readers know it, and we can only conclude that Joseph is not, in the end, displaying a selfish kind of meanness.

Joseph is testing their words for truth value. After all, they claimed that they were honest and upright men! They can easily "talk the talk," but have their lives in the past been honest and upright? We readers know otherwise, and Joseph knows otherwise. So, Joseph had said in verses 15 and 16 that he would put them through a test, an ordeal, to see whether their talk was genuine or whether it was just so much "hot air."

Joseph has two purposes in all this testing:

1. He is testing the ten men to see if a genuine *attitude* of remorse and repentance is alive in their souls. Do they see how awful their sin against Joseph had been?
2. He is also testing his brothers to see if there are *actions* of repentance as well. Will they follow through and own up to their responsibilities by bringing forth fruits that go with repentance? For example, will they later abandon Benjamin? Time will tell.

Thus Joseph's whole treatment of his ten brothers serves as a kind of sifting, a form of discipline. While Jacob does not know their crime (although he may be suspicious), Joseph does knows it. By placing their money back in their grain, he has given them a trial in a kind of "take-home test." The discovery of the money serves only to keep the agitation alive in their hearts and consciences. The goal is spiritually therapeutic: if they allow their real guilt to come to the surface where they might deal with it, the healing of their hearts and their spiritual growth in holiness might move forward. If Christians wish to live and die in the joy of their only comfort of belonging to Jesus Christ, they must first know how great their sin and misery really is (see Heidelberg Catechism, Lord's Day 1, Q&A 2). Then the splendor of grace in Christ appear so radiant and

amazing. And then we are free to live the new life of
thanksgiving in the joy and power of Christ's Holy Spirit.

The knowledge of God's grace is never well-known unless
there is a right knowledge of our own sin and misery.
The flood of joy comes when it breaks through our sin and
into our dull hearts. Unconditional election by God is not
the sovereign call in grace of those people who by nature
are good, but of those people who are unrighteous.
God justifies the ungodly (Rom. 4:5). Consider the power
of these passages:

1. Luke 7:47: Jesus tells the Pharisee Simon, "Her many sins
   have been forgiven—for she loved much. But he who has
   been forgiven little loves little." Horrible sins are dealt
   with by means of even greater grace, and that in turn
   draws out of us even greater love.
2. 1 Corinthians 6:9–11: Paul reminds us that the wicked
   will not inherit the kingdom of God. He also notes that
   through God's grace "such were some of you."
   A genuine change takes place in the lives of God's elect
   so that they are washed, sanctified, and justified "in the
   name of the Lord Jesus Christ and by the Spirit of
   our God." Grace overcomes any kind of sin, even those
   that are so disgusting.

Ephesians 2:8–10: there is no room for human boasting,
since salvation is by grace alone, not upon the basis of
human works. Sin prevents our good works, even our best
works, from ever being the reason that we are saved.
Instead, we are God's workmanship, created for those good
works in Christ Jesus. Grace alone is the firm foundation
for a healthy life of good works.

Points to Ponder and Discuss

1. Jacob says to his sons, "You have deprived me of my children. Joseph is no more…" How might that statement have affected these sons? Did this likely press the test of conscience even more for them? Could they now wonder if their father is suspicious about their involvement in the disappearance of Joseph?

2. Joseph has put his brothers on a kind of trial, and these are men guilty of heinous crimes. We want judges, juries, and the court system to be just. However, if we are the ones aggrieved, how easy is it for feelings of revenge to take over? Do we rejoice when the guilty are found guilty? What role does mercy play in the whole question of administering justice?

3. What is meant by "cheap grace"? If Joseph had simply welcomed his brothers with a "let bygones be bygones" attitude, would that have been cheap grace? Would there still be important matters unresolved?

4. Read Psalm 32. What does it say about the sinner when he does not confess his sins? What are the blessings of confession? Isn't confession "good for the soul"?

5. Why do people allow sins to go so long without confession? What happens in families in such cases?

Lesson 11

Israel's Sons Return to Egypt with Benjamin

Read Genesis 43

Introduction

In Genesis 42 the sons of Jacob go to Egypt for food since the famine has hit Canaan very hard. Joseph recognizes them, and he recalls the message of his dreams. He initiates a process of testing his brothers by accusing them of being spies, imprisoning them for three days, but then sending them home. He keeps Simeon in custody, telling them they may return to Egypt only if the youngest brother comes with them. He is testing them to see if they are honest men. In fact, this test stirs up feelings of guilt as they remember what they had done to Joseph many years earlier. Even more astonishing to them is finding their money—all their money—returned in the grain sacks they brought back from Egypt! What is God doing to them?

Genesis 43 tells us about the brothers' second visit to Egypt. Actually this visit will last through chapter 45, since their return home in Genesis 44 will be interrupted when the Egyptians discover the silver cup in the sack of Benjamin, and the brothers are brought back to Joseph for judgment. This second visit to Egypt will be amazing in terms of the many things (and people) that will be revealed.

Continuing Stress in Israel's Family (43:1–14)

The famine has dragged on, and food resources become scarce. Israel's pantry begins to thin out. We wonder whether Israel was even able to keep many (or all) of his own servants, since there are many mouths to feed in his household. Israel (the name used for Jacob in this chapter, the name he had received from the wrestling "stranger in the night") presses his sons to return to Egypt for food. Actually, the family discussions take up the first 14 verses of this chapter, and the things they discuss are basically a repeat (with some variations) of several things mentioned in Genesis 42:30–34. Judah emerges here as the chief spokesman in talking with his father.

We have not been impressed with Judah up to this point. Judah was the brother who suggested that they sell Joseph and profit financially from their collective hatred of him. Judah then leaves the family circle, marries a Canaanite, and he begins building his own family. He appears to blame Tamar for his sons' deaths, he visits without qualms a prostitute, but he is righteously indignant when his daughter-in-law Tamar is pregnant through prostitution. Yet, for all that, the statement he makes when he is confronted with the sure evidence that he is the father of Tamar's children— "She is more righteous than I"—suggests that there may be some change in his own heart. Maybe, just maybe, the Holy Spirit has begun to work in Judah's heart so that his life begins to take a new direction. The twins born at the end of Genesis 38 are named Perez and Zerah. Perez means "breakthrough," and Zerah means "dawn." Has God broken through to Judah, got his attention, so that a new chapter in his life might be dawning?

We do not read of Judah again until the family is hungry, and the sons of Israel must visit Egypt to get grain. Reuben still feels guilt. What about Judah? What are his thoughts and his attitudes about what had happened to Joseph? What will Judah's actions be?

Judah points out the great dilemma that Israel's family now faces. In verses 3–5 Judah begins and ends his words by reminding his father, "The man solemnly warned us, 'You will not see my face again unless your brother is with you.'" Either Benjamin comes along, or the family of Israel faces slow starvation. Israel lashes out by accusing his sons of telling something they should not have mentioned. But hindsight is always 20/20, and the principle of unintended consequences seems to apply. Is father Israel being unfair to his sons? While he does not know the precise role his sons have played in the disappearance of Joseph, he is desperate to hold onto Benjamin. But the brothers can claim, with some legitimacy, that they had no idea that the questioning by "the man" in Egypt would lead to him making this demand: "Either the young brother comes along, or you can forget about ever getting food from me again." The family is caught between the proverbial "rock and a hard place." But the sons of Israel are caught between two other hard places: the harsh words and demand of the "the man" in Egypt, on the one hand, and the painful lament of their father, on the other hand.

Judah's speech is very striking in verses 8–10. While we cannot be sure that he is speaking for all his brothers at this point in terms of attitude and purpose, we stand amazed that Judah readily promises to protect his half-brother Benjamin. Judah assumes full responsibility for his well-being, and if he should fail, Judah accepts the fact that the blame and guilt for failure will be his alone.

Being Afraid in Joseph's House (43:15–25)

The text is deliberate in telling us what the brothers take to Egypt: gifts, twice the amount of money, and Benjamin. They also go with their father's prayer: "May God Almighty (*El-Shaddai*) grant you mercy before the man…" All of these will play a role in terms of satisfying "the man." But it is the sight of Benjamin (verse 16) that prompts Joseph to move to another phase of his test. No longer will they be subjected to intense questioning, but they will be his guests at a feast in Joseph's house.

All that the brothers know is that they have been summoned to the man's house. They fear the worst. They recognize their own helplessness, complete vulnerability, before Joseph. That "the man" might actually love them as a true brother is the last thing in their minds. They think that he remembers the "lost" money (found in their grain sacks), and now he is vengeful, fully prepared to sell them into slavery and confiscate their donkeys. Ironic, isn't it: these brothers, who had sold Joseph into slavery, are now afraid that "the man" will sell them into slavery. They are feeling anxiety similar to what their young brother Joseph had experienced years earlier.

Joseph Treats His Brothers to a Banquet (43:26–34)

Joseph arrives at home, and the terrified sons of Israel can only act in a very careful manner to show their deep humility. These are the brave men who had earlier mocked Joseph as the "lord of dreams, that dreamer" (Gen. 37:19). They were prepared to kill him, and they thought nothing of selling him to strangers in a murderous attempt to be rid of him. But now, they are reduced to cowering in his presence. Twice the text tells us (verses 26, 28) that they bowed down before him, further serving to fulfill the dream prophecies of Genesis 37.

Joseph almost seems to be playing the so-called "good cop, bad cop" game with them. In the first visit, he makes a strong accusation against them ("You're all spies!"), but he then releases them to go home with grain. Their money mysteriously (at least it is mysterious to them) appears in their sacks, prompting them to think that God had miraculously put it there. When they are ordered to Joseph's house, they fear the worst, but when they are there, they are given water to wash their feet and food for their donkeys.

We might think that Joseph is toying with their emotions, "playing with their heads," so to speak. The net effect that Joseph intends is for them to be kept off-guard. At the same time, it may be that he has approved and appreciates their honesty in that they did do what he had required of them: they have brought Benjamin with them. So, he now wants to feast with them, although they will not yet know the reason why.

Here then is another irony: while Joseph had pleaded with them from the pit, they had eaten a meal, completely indifferent to his cries (Gen. 37:25). But now, Joseph serves them a feast, arranging them in seating order according to their ages, oldest to the youngest. This "man" must have divine knowledge!

The brothers can only look on with more wonderment at the fact that the youngest, Benjamin, gets five times as much as they received. Why him? What is Joseph's strategy here? There may be several things going on here at once. First, it may be simply Joseph's sheer pleasure at seeing his brother again, that, though Joseph must remain incognito, he can at least show this kindness by giving his younger brother plenty to eat and drink. People like to see those they love satisfied with good food. But secondly, this may be a subtle "special coat" strategy. Just as the special coat that Jacob had given young Joseph created jealousy and hatred from Joseph's brothers, so it may be that Joseph will pile on the benefits to Benjamin as a way to stir up whatever sinful attitudes and dark feelings that may be lingering below the surface in the half-brothers' hearts. If Benjamin gets special treatment, how will they all look upon him then? Will it be something like this, "There it is again! Another son of Rachel gets treated better than we." If Joseph has this in mind, then he is further working toward his brothers' refinement. Joseph is not tempting them to sin, but he is testing them. Once more, time will tell what really lives in their hearts.

Points to Ponder and Discuss

1. Judah seems to have replaced Reuben as the leader of Israel's sons. Reuben had offered two of his sons to be killed if Benjamin is not brought back home (Gen. 42:37). But Judah offers himself (Gen. 43:9, 10). Is Reuben falling to the background because of his earlier sin with Bilhah (Gen. 35:22), or because he was ineffectual as the firstborn son when he failed to protect Joseph? What has happened to Judah that might explain this change in him?

2. All of us probably know of people who show indifference or even contempt for the things of the Lord and His Kingdom in their early years. Perhaps we may have been like that ourselves. The early Judah strikes us as cold and calculating. Is it too easy for more mature Christians to give up on prodigal sons and daughters of the covenant? Is there ever a point when we may give up on them? What things can we do to keep up meaningful Christian contact and witness with them?

3. Father Israel finally sends his sons to Egypt with the prayer that God Almighty may grant them mercy before "the man." Is prayer a last resort for Israel? How do faith and trust interrelate with planning and careful thinking? How will God's power and mercy play out in this story?

4. Joseph was called "the man who is over the land" earlier, but in Genesis 43 he is typically called "the man." From "the man" the brothers have experienced forms of judgment (accusation, imprisonment) as well as mercy (food, returned money, freedom to go home). Like it or not, the sons of Israel must deal with "the man." To what extent do these things anticipate the (royal, kingly) work of the Lord Jesus Christ later on in history? How is Christ involved with us in both judgment and in mercy?

5. Judah's speech is so striking in terms of what he is willing to risk for both his father and his half-brother. He is willing to take responsibility for a brother, and he is prepared to assume guilt in the matter. Later on Christ is made like His brothers in every way in order to be a sympathetic High Priest for us. In what ways does Judah's speech here anticipate the (priestly) work of the Lord Jesus Christ later? What will Christ actually do to be responsible for us? What does He do with our own guilt?

6. The brothers recognizing and not recognizing one another provides us readers some very powerful drama in this story. In addition, meals play a key role at certain moments in redemptive-history. Contrast this all with great meal in the new creation, the marriage supper of the Lamb (Rev. 19:9). What will be the mutual recognition of Christ and of each other that will occur in the new heavens and new earth? How does Jesus Christ treat us now, and how will He treat us who were once His enemies?

Joseph "Arrests" His Brothers

Read Genesis 44:1–17

Introduction

There were some tense moments for Israel's sons as their
shopping trip for food had begun, especially when Joseph's
steward directed them to Joseph's house. They feared the
worst, proclaimed their innocence, showed him the money,
and offered the gifts. Lots of bowing did not hurt their
cause either. But in the end, Joseph hosts his brothers and
some Egyptians at a feast. The tensions melt away as food
is consumed and drink is imbibed. Everyone is left feeling
really good as evening falls, and the brothers then sleep,
intending to return home in the morning.

Joseph Plans to Trap His Brothers (44:1–5)

Joseph works together with his own steward in order to set
up this "sting operation." This is not quite the same thing as
entrapment, in which a person will be tempted to commit
a crime. Rather, Joseph wants a situation to be set up that
will extend his test of his brothers. They have claimed to be
innocent men, and he has overheard the brief discussion they
had about guilt (Gen. 42:21, 22). They have *talked* a
good line: do they walk the same good line? Joseph's plan
will serve to uncover what is really going on in their hearts.

Joseph tells his steward to fill their grain sacks generously
("as much food as they can carry"). He will appear good
beyond expectations. But into the sacks will go their money
(again!), and his own silver cup will go into Benjamin's sack.
The beloved son of father Israel either will be the object of

the brothers' protection, or, he will be another brother
abandoned to his fate in Egypt. Which will it be? Time will tell.
Joseph is testing them.

The brothers had partied with Joseph the day before, and
the night of sleep now has passed. The donkeys are loaded
with grain, and they set out on the way home. We can only
imagine that the men must have felt great relief and even
joy for the most recent events. Consider this: the harsh ruler
who controlled the grain had released Simeon and even
hosted them at a feast. He had acted so kindly to Benjamin,
the young brother concerning whom all in the family
had worried. Obviously this harsh ruler has softened
toward these men from Canaan, and their actions had
proven that they were innocent men, honest men.
Taking Benjamin along, although a gamble (humanly
speaking), had paid off The donkeys were loaded down
with grain for the household in Canaan. Father Israel
would see all of his living sons again (Simeon and Benjamin
included), and there was plenty of groceries as well. Does it
get better than this?

However, this delightfully pleasant picture will end
very soon. Joseph is scripting the events as they unfold; he
knows what he is doing. Probably the evening before,
Joseph's steward is given his lines with which to confront
the men. They are to be accused of stealing a very personal
item that Joseph uses, his silver cup. This theft is described
as repaying good with evil. The master of the steward has
shown such great kindness and hospitality to these foreigner
visitors, and now look what they have done: stolen this
special cup! It is ironic that the brothers had earlier sold
Joseph to the Midianite merchants for silver. Now they
will be accused of stealing silver in the form of a cup.
Some scholars think that this silver cup was no small object,
perhaps something approaching the size of a punch-bowl
(see Currid, *Genesis*, II:310).

The term "divination" is used in verse 5. Some pagan cultures would read omens by pouring water and oil into such sacred cups (bowls) and then studying how the liquids flowed or mixed together. This is something on the order of reading animal entrails or watching the flight of birds. Stealing such an object was viewed as a very serious crime, the penalty for which could be either death or being reduced to a slave. It is most likely that Joseph is playing a role here and not actually one who used such divination.

Joseph's Steward "Finds" the Silver Cup (44:6–13)

The steward easily overtakes the men, who have not traveled a great distance at all. Hearing these charges, the brothers immediately proclaim their innocence. "Not guilty!" is their plea. They are prepared to make a vigorous defense. They remind the steward that they had brought the silver back from Canaan. Who would have ever expected them to do something like that? If they had gone to such extremes over the earlier cash they had found in their sacks, then surely no one could accuse them of taking anything from the Egyptian ruler. So certain are the brothers of their innocence that they pronounce their own sentence: the guilty person should be executed, while all the rest of the brothers could be reduced to slavery. Obviously they must have all proclaimed their innocence before any search has started. "Not me! I don't have this silver cup." With this their sure belief, would the brothers have dared to pronounce such a possible sentence against themselves?

It is noteworthy, however, that the Egyptian steward lightens the sentence. He says in verse 10 that the guilty man would become a slave, while the rest would be free from blame. The possibility of escape from judgment is held up at this point, but it is only a moot point here: the brothers are convinced that no silver cup will be found. So, what difference does it make to talk about any possible punishment?

The sacks are quickly unloaded from the donkeys. The steward also knows in what order to proceed: start with the oldest brother and move toward the "guilty" one, the youngest. The text says nothing about any of their money being found: the object of the search—and thus of narrative and dramatic tension—is the silver cup. We suspect that each brother breathes a sigh of relief, or perhaps feels (maybe says?), "See, I told you so," when no cup is found in his sack.

There is another irony in this story, a parallel from an earlier incident. When Jacob had left his father-in-law Laban in Genesis 31, Laban is outraged that Jacob has left with his (stolen?) daughters, Jacob's wives, Leah and Rachel. Laban is also very upset that his teraphim were taken, and he searches the group to find these teraphim. Jacob does not know that Rachel has them in a saddle-bag on her camel, just as the brothers were very unaware that the silver cup is in Benjamin's grain sack. One difference, of course, is that Laban never finds the stolen teraphim as Rachel remains seated. But the Egyptian steward, Joseph's accomplice in this sting, finds the "missing" silver cup. Jacob had been allowed to depart with Leah and Rachel, but the brothers of Joseph will not be so fortunate. When the last grain sack is searched, the cup is found.

At this point, the brothers feel the world collapsing around them. Shocked and numb with grief and disbelief, they tear their clothes. Reuben had done the same thing years earlier when he came back to his brothers, only to find that Joseph was sold and therefore gone (Gen. 37:29). Here, all the brothers tear their clothes, a symbolic action as if to say that their world has "come apart" as emotional pain rips through their hearts. They have no choice: they are under arrest, so to speak, since the steward has undoubtedly come out with some armed guards. They must return to the city and face "the man," the owner of the silver cup.

Joseph Offers His Brothers a Plea Bargain (44:14–17)

When listening to news stories about people arrested and accused, we often hear about prosecutors offering a plea bargain arrangement with the accused. The prosecution may lessen the charge in order to get a conviction. The brothers had been so confident of their collective innocence that they were ready to call upon themselves harsh penalties (verse 9). Even the steward had said such was not necessary: only the guilty would be the slave, while the rest could continue on their journey home.

The issue in this portion of Scripture is the fate of Benjamin. What will happen to him? And with that, what role, if any, will the other sons of Israel play in whatever happens to Benjamin? The arrest is part of the test: what kind of men are they now? In earlier audiences, the men had bowed in proper Near Eastern fashion as subjects before a mighty ruler. But in verse 14 they simply fall to the ground, men reduced to utter helplessness. They literally throw themselves upon the mercy of the court.

Joseph proceeds to give them a tongue-lashing about their crime of stealing, suggesting that he was able to discover their guilt by divination. The brothers had witnessed the incredible ability of Joseph to seat them according to birth order and age; it is believable to hear him say that he could know who the "guilty" party is. And yet, they all know this simple fact: *they did not steal the cup.* How in the world will they be able to convince "the man" that they really are innocent?

Do not fail to notice the man that is quietly identified as the leader of the brothers. Reuben, Simeon, and Levi are not the apparent leaders. Verse 14 says, "Judah and his brothers came in." It is Judah, the fourth son, who leads in making the opening remarks for the defense (verse 16). Judah continues to emerge in the story as the son on the rise. This will set the stage for the speech that Judah will give during this trial Joseph has with these men.

Judah says "we." He mentions "your servants' guilt," using the plural. He states the verdict: "*we* are now my lord's slaves," again speaking in the plural. But Joseph suggests, "Let's make a deal." He proposes that it would be unjust to enslave them all. No, only the guilty should have to pay. He shows them all an open door: you're all free to go home in peace. Only the guilty brother, Benjamin, will stay behind as a slave. Joseph does not say that he will execute Benjamin. Will the brothers take this bait? Will they escape, coming home (again) with another son of beloved Rachel missing? What does love demand in such a case? Being filled with terror and with a desire to survive and live, what might they do? What would you do?

Points to Ponder and Discuss

1. Joseph knows that his brothers have a strong sense of guilt about what they had done to him many years earlier. But he sees that they did what he demanded, namely, they have brought young brother Benjamin along. So, why does Joseph keep up this bit of a charade? Why does he not reveal himself to his brothers now? What more does he need to know about his brothers?

2. Joseph's brothers are not sinless men, but they are not guilty of the theft of which they are accused. What does the Scripture teach us about God's people being falsely accused? How should we respond in such circumstances? (Think of the many Psalms that address this; e.g., Psalms 26, 28, 44, etc.)

3. Joseph tests his brothers so that they might show what is really in their hearts at this point in redemptive-history. How is this similar to the test that righteous Job suffers? Does the Lord allow such tests today in the lives of some

of His saints? Eventually the brothers find out who is testing them. Does Job ever get a similar insight on why he suffers and is tested as he is?

4. Collective guilt and individual responsibility: how are these two elements at work in this story? How do they play out in other places in redemptive history? Read Ezekiel 18.

5. The brothers are terrified by the judgment that may be brought against them. In the Garden of Gethsemane, Christ also faced the utter horror and terror of God's awesome justice against sin. He faced hellish agony on the Cross. What did Christ pray then? What did He do there for us?

Lesson 13

Judah Intercedes for Benjamin

Read Genesis 44:18–34

Introduction

During the first visit of Joseph's ten brothers to Egypt,
they claimed that they were "honest men" (Gen. 42:11).
Joseph recognized them and remembered the dreams of
his youth. He then proceeds to test them to see whether their
claim to be honest men was true (Gen. 42:15, 16).
But Joseph's interest is more than whether they were honest
in their words at the present moment. What kind of men are
they now, years after the tragic events in which they had
plotted murder and then sold Joseph into slavery? Had they
changed, or were they even more hardened in their sinful
hatred and cruelty? Joseph overhears them say that God had
exposed their guilt. But now the test that Joseph puts them
through will reveal whether they are changed in terms of how
they will act. Joseph secretly has planted his own silver cup in
the grain sack of his brother Benjamin. Will the brothers defend
Benjamin, or will they abandon him to his fate?

Joseph awaited the return of his official, the man sent out
to stop the brothers on their way home. The plan is
working out as he had anticipated. The cup was found in
Benjamin's sack of grain. The brothers are not prepared to
fight back against the Egyptian authorities. They have torn
their clothes in shock and grief, and they silently return to
Joseph's house where they throw themselves to the ground.
Joseph stays in character as the harsh official, the man who
has accused them, imprisoned them, released them, and also

feasted with them. He roughly accuses them again, suggesting that he knows more than an ordinary mortal might know.

Judah faces this harsh man with no plea, pained by the knowledge that they are all innocent. How can their innocence be proved? On the other hand, the evidence against them was clearly found in Benjamin's sack. "God has uncovered your servants' guilt. We are now my lord's slaves" (verse 17). This is the situation in Judah's mind. In other words, we will all suffer the sentence together.

Joseph counters with a kind of bargain for the brothers to take, and, on the surface of things, a bargain that is truly merciful: only the guilty man, Benjamin, should pay for the crime and not the entire group. This is quite a merciful offer from such an important Egyptian official, from the same man who had accused them of being spies before. He is showing the ten brothers an open door that will allow them to escape slavery in Egypt. No money to bribe the official. No "community service" to perform in some Egyptian city. Just go home!

Again, from a truly selfish vantage point, the picture presented by Joseph is clear. Self-interest would whisper in the fearful, anxious hearts of the brothers, "Let's get out of here! The man is prepared to let us go. Let's get out while the 'getting' is good, before this guy changes his mind." They have now every opportunity to abandon Benjamin. They could now all get away now with their lives. Will they take this opportunity to save their own skins? Here is the test.

Judah Recalls the Events to This Point (44:18–30)

Genesis 44:18–34 is a very moving and passionate defense of Benjamin. It is as moving as the following scene in Genesis 45 in which Joseph reveals himself to his brothers. Judah and his brothers cannot argue justice, but only mercy. Judah is almost eloquent as he begins with words that border on flattery. Joseph is addressed repeatedly as "my lord" while the brothers are referred to as "your servants." All of this is in line with the language style of the ancient Near East. He seeks to soften up the harsh official. We the readers, however, must be clear as to what Judah's purpose is here. He is not seeking to have the harsh Egyptian lord release him and his "non-guilty" brothers. Joseph has said that he may go! Rather, Judah is trying to have Benjamin set free. That is the sole issue that Judah must address.

Judah's emotional address to Joseph reveals to him what the "official story" had been about his death earlier: he had been torn to pieces. Furthermore, Judah's appeal contains a few minor differences with what we have read earlier. For example, Judah says that Joseph had asked about a father and a brother. But in Genesis 42:13 we read that the brothers had mentioned their father and brother, apparently unasked. Also, earlier the brothers had said that one brother is "no more." In Genesis 44:20, Judah says that he is "dead." (Quite a surprise: Joseph knows that reports of his death are greatly exaggerated...but Judah does not yet know that!).

In this speech of Judah, Joseph learns about the painful reaction of his father Jacob to both the demand that Benjamin come along as well as Jacob's reaction to the loss of Joseph, 22 years earlier (verses 24–29). We can read of Jacob's earlier reactions in Genesis 42:36–38; 43:6; and 43:11–14. In the speech, Judah mentions his father 14 times! Jacob had loved Joseph, and Joseph knew it. They all knew it!

There are three points in Judah's most moving intercession, as he pleads to suffer in Benjamin's place. Judah recalls the facts leading to Benjamin's coming to Egypt. We learn (again) the facts that led to the present situation, we hear what effect there will be on father Jacob if Benjamin does not return, and we hear of Judah's firm vow to take the younger brother's place.

Judah Details the Possible Effects on Jacob (44:30, 31)

Judah spells out how the father's love for Benjamin is like two lives that have become intertwined. If the one is gone, the other will fade away in grief and sorrow. Joseph must have heard these words and remembered Jacob's love for him in earlier years. Thus Joseph knows that Jacob has transferred that same love and affection upon Benjamin. Losing Joseph had been hard enough; losing Benjamin will be fatal, according to Judah.

What has gotten into Judah to say all this? He has really changed! Judah accepts God's ways in exposing their guilt (verse 16). Compare this with the earlier Judah (Gen. 37:26, 27). Joseph now knows that the brother who sold him into slavery has become a brother willing to assume slavery rather than cause the death of his father. Once an enemy, Judah has become a true "brother." This point is critical for all that happens next. Clearly Judah emerges now as an intercessor who is willing to assume the fate of his brother. Compare this with what Christ did (Phil. 2:5–11) when He emptied Himself of heavenly glory and assumed servant form and willingly died a cursed death in our place.

Clearly, Judah has accepted the fact that Benjamin has replaced Joseph as his father's favorite son. No bitterness, no jealousy, and no hatred against Benjamin are evident. This is quite remarkable, but it is something for which we readers can give God alone the glory. The emphasis should not be first of all on Judah, his honesty or even his bravery. Rather, such a transformation of heart and attitude in Judah comes about only through the quiet yet powerful working of the Holy Spirit of Jesus Christ.

Judah Vows to Take Benjamin's Place (44:32–34)

Judah is being true to his word, since he had vowed that he personally would act to defend the safety of Benjamin (see Gen. 43:9, 10). There is some irony here in that it was Judah who had earlier proposed selling Joseph into slavery (see Gen. 37:27). Now Judah stands before that same brother, only now Judah is offering himself as a slave to Joseph. The tables are turned!

By nature, we are selfish, considering "number one" ("Me, myself, and I") to be the center of the universe and therefore the focus of reality. By nature, we are absorbed in ourselves, and the concerns of others are not our primary concern. Judah, like his other brothers, hated Joseph and was prepared to kill him. But he has changed: now he is fully prepared to give up his own life for Joseph's younger brother, Benjamin. This change comes by God's amazing grace!

The character of Judah's offer of himself stands in stark contrast with what Reuben had earlier proposed. Reuben had earlier offered his two sons, proposing that they die if Reuben failed to protect Benjamin (Gen. 42:37). That is, "let me—Reuben—live, but you can kill my two sons." That is a rather sorry offer! Jacob could not bear to lose Benjamin *and* watch two grandsons also be put death. But Judah does not offer anyone else—just himself.

A later son of Judah, Jesus Christ, would do something like that. "For God loved the world in this way: He gave His only begotten Son…" (John 3:16). That verse, which we all know and love so much, puts before us the great reality that God sent His own and only Son, not someone else's son. For there was no other because there could be no other to accomplish what needed to be done in order to rescue and redeem those who were under a death sentence. After Adam and Eve rebelled against God their Father in the Garden of Eden, the entire world and all of mankind stood under a death sentence. Humanity was condemned to death. But the gospel announces that God the Father sent God the Son into this world, not to condemn it, but to redeem it by His blood (see John 3:17). He gave His life as a substitute for us, purchasing all those whom God had chosen in electing love before the foundation of heaven and earth (see Eph. 1:3ff.).

"Greater love has no man than this, that he lay down his life for his friends" (John 15:13). Judah refuses to leave Benjamin to a future of slavery and thus watch his father die in soul-crushing grief. Judah declares that he will trade his life for his half-brother. Judah's speech shatters Joseph. His demeanor breaks, for he hears the very words that only come from a man changed by something far greater than human "niceness." Judah has been changed by the Spirit of his even greater descendant, his Son Jesus Christ.

Points to Ponder and Discuss

1. Why does Judah take the lead here in speaking to Joseph? Why do Reuben and the other brothers seem to fall silent?
2. Judah and his brothers experience a kind of "judgment day" when they appear before Joseph to give an answer for the accusation of stealing a special silver cup. They throw themselves on the "mercy of the court." Hebrews 9:27 says that man is "destined to die once, and after that to face judgment." What is the only hope for believers in that great day of days when we must all appear before God in judgment? How can God be merciful to us then?
3. The dilemma the brothers face when Joseph offers them an escape—but in the process they would abandon Benjamin—is one Christians often face. It is easy to confess love and loyalty to Jesus Christ on Sundays when surrounded by fellow believers, but how do we confess him in the areas of life outside of the comfortable church circles? What kinds of challenges do you face at work or in school in which it is very difficult to confess Christ?

4. Judah is prepared to defend Benjamin from slavery. Later, Peter in the upper room was prepared to die for Christ. But he wilted later when he stood in the courtyard of the high priest, and people pointed at him as a follower of Christ. Why did Peter's faith falter at that point? From where does true Christian courage come?

5. The Apostle John writes in 1 John 4:16, "This is how we know what love is: Jesus Christ laid down His life for us. And we ought to lay down our lives for our brothers." This suggests that our love for one another should be prepared to go as far as martyrdom. But, since most of us will not be confronted with that extreme sacrifice, how do we show the same kind of love today to brothers and sisters in the faith?

Group 1

1 Andrew & Anita Zuidhof
2 Roeline Bennan
3 Dick & Sharon Dalhuisen
4 Brian & Emily Makkinga
5 David & Karen Linker
6 Scott Rypstra
7 Sarris & Corry Vander Scheer
8 Martin & Gaylene Van de Pol
9 Murray & Annette Wiersma
10 Leanna Walls
11 Matt & Daisy Fraser
12 Rebecca Bevaart

Group 2

1 Kevin & Nicole Tolsma
2 Garth & Evelyn Pol
3 Rev. Barry & Val Beukema
4 Michael Makkinga
5 Sarah Linker
6 Amy Stiksma
7 Bertus & Gerda Van Ginkel
8 Jason & Jessica Vander Woerd
9 Karissa Zuidhof
10 Jeff & Michelle Van Olst
11 Robert & Kim Walls
12 Norman Walls

Group 3

1 Pete & Lisa Ellens
2 Jonathan & Michelle Bevaart
3 Jeremy & Jacqueline Dalhuisen
4 Randy Makkinga
5 Aaron & Miranda Beukema
6 Tyson & Gwen Tiggelaar
7 Marco & Bonnie Van't Klooster
8 Dyron & Leanne Provost
9 Julia Zuidhof
10 Kevin & Becky Kooiker
11 Evert & Betty Van de Pol
12 Peter & Shannon Luong

Group 4

1 Brian & Sharon Bevaart
2 Ryan & Amy Bultena
3 Siemon & Irene Feitsma
4 Mark & Christina Makkinga
5 Darren & Christine Van Gelderen
6 Brian & Briana Van de Pol
7 Henry & Grace Visser
8 Robert Van Ginkel
9 Erin Wiersma
10 Edwin & Alison Niemeijer
11 Nathan Van de Pol
12 Rob & Michelle DeRegt

Group 5

1 Gerry & Wilma Makkinga
2 Trevor Ellens
3 Sarah Beukema
4 Kevin & Maria Makkinga
5 Wim & Nita Floryn
6 Rachel Van de Pol
7 Wim & Sylvia Schakel
8 Mark & Gerlinde Visser
9 Pete & Joanne Walls
10 Stuart & Kelsie Wiersma
11 Wietse & Catherine Jagersma

Group 7 (Seniors)

1 Egbert & Minke Breukelman
2 Arie & Marion de Boon
3 Garritt & Diane Pikkert
4 Margaret Pol
5 Helen Pikkert
6 Sam Salomons
7 Anne Siebenga
8 Sue Stevens
9 Klaas & Ann Tiemstra
10 Margaret Van Haren

* Bible Study is held the 2nd & 4th Wednesday of each month starting on October 23th
** The first lesson will be at the home of the first person on your group's list

Joseph Reveals Himself to His Brothers

Read Genesis 45:1–11

Introduction

The speech of Judah put in front of Joseph a picture of a family going through misery and distress. Joseph has been testing his brothers, but the dramatic and moving speech of Judah is the "final exam" in this test. Joseph now knows that his brothers (at least Judah, but surely the same is true for the others) have changed. They have grown in God's grace and knowledge as the Holy Spirit has been working in their collective hearts. They freely admit guilt, and they will not seek the easy way out by quickly exiting the court where Joseph is judge in order to flee to the safety of Canaan but abandon Benjamin in the process. Love is not merely an emotional attachment; it is seen as giving oneself. Judah pledges that he will give himself in the place of Benjamin. Judah cannot bear to see Benjamin lost to slavery and thus bring his aged father Jacob to the grave in abject misery, broken-hearted.

Joseph, the Weeping Patriarch (45:1–3)

Few people can read this story themselves without being moved deeply in their souls. Joseph's tears of joy are an expression of the pain, the love, the affection, and the reconciliation that has been welling up in his soul, only waiting for the right moment to express it. Now the opportunity has presented itself, and Joseph this time does

---

not walk quickly into another room in order to have a good cry. He has wept on two other occasions. The first time that he had wept was when he heard Reuben chastise his brothers for sinning against him (see Gen. 42:22–24). Joseph gets the first inkling that there is some sense of guilt among his brothers (at least, with the eldest). The second time was when Joseph sets his eyes upon his younger brother Benjamin during the brothers' second visit to Egypt to get food (see Gen. 43:30). On both of these earlier occasions, Joseph had to make an emotional recovery, wash his face, and thus continue to hide from his brothers what he knows (and what we readers know): the brothers are all together physically, yet Joseph is hid from their eyes, but in time they will be united again in heart. But now Joseph's emotional outburst is like the bursting of the proverbial dam so that all the feelings that have welled up in him, may come out. They then hear words that leave them all speechless, "I am Joseph."

Joseph Reveals God's Plan in All This (45:4–13)

Joseph's speech is also eloquent in its own way. He is not only over them in terms of power, but he reveals himself to be advanced in knowledge of the ways of God. Perhaps the years of separation from his family in Canaan have given him the occasions to think about the big picture of what is going on in all of this. Again, perhaps the sight of his own brothers bowing down to him, a sight that recalls his own prophetic dreams (see Gen. 42:9), has spurred his reflections in an even sharper way to reflect on how the hand of God must be involved in all this. Consider this: if the dreams come from God, then they were prophetic. The message in the two dreams would be that Joseph at some point in time would have authority over his brothers, and he would rule them. But who would have imagined that being a ruler over the brothers would mean that Joseph would have to

undergo a couple of near-death experiences! First, in a pit
in Canaan, and then in the royal "pit" (prison) in
Egypt, Joseph escapes death, certain death in any other
set of circumstances.

But God had now elevated him to a key position in Egypt,
controlling the food supply that would feed people both far
and near. Joseph describes himself as "father to Pharaoh"
(verse 8), an honorary title apparently that indicates Joseph,
although young, is a very important advisor to the ruler of
Egypt (like a chief of staff to a national leader). Even more
than that, Joseph *rules* Egypt under Pharaoh! God must
have done all this. Looking back upon all these events,
Joseph is given insight by God to see that this is not random
chance, and it is not fickle "good luck." Not at all!
Three times (see verses 5, 7, and 8) Joseph tells his brothers
that God had sent him ahead of them in order to save many
people alive. In other words, we may say that God was
working through events that from one angle surely are evil
and wicked, but in the divine plan, these events and actions
will serve to keep the church of God alive. Joseph is a kind
of Noah (on a smaller scale), a man used by God to
preserve life, the life of His people.

Joseph uses words that have the effect of binding him
again to his family. He refers to "my father," calls himself
"your brother" or (in reference to Jacob), "your son."
His goal is reconciliation and reunion with his family.
He has seen his brothers; all that is left to complete this
cozy picture is for Joseph to see his aged father again.
So, he tells them to return quickly (see verses 9, 13) to
Canaan, in order to bring father Jacob and the entire clan
of Israel to Egypt.

Joseph also shows true empathy with his brothers since he
knows what it must mean in their troubled hearts now to
realize that the brother they had once tried to remove, once
and for all, now stands before them with the power of life

Forgiveness, empathy, and knowledge of the future. Joseph shows this last item as well. He knows that there will be five more years of famine, not because he uses a silver cup to predict the future and not because he has better insight into long term weather patterns or how the Nile River will (or will not) flood. He tells his brothers exactly how long the famine will be because the Lord has revealed that important fact to him. Joseph knows where he can settle his family, once they all get back to Egypt: they will live in the region of Goshen, and Joseph will provide for them, just as he provided for all Egypt. Here is the choice: life in Egypt under Joseph's care, or destitution, poverty, and much hunger in Canaan.

Joseph's Brothers: Terror, Then Tears (45:3, 14, 15)

Joseph's brothers have been on an emotional roller-coaster in all their dealings with this harsh ruler, and this scene of personal full disclosure is no different. We can only wonder what thoughts are racing through their hearts and minds as they hear Joseph bark out the order, "Everybody out!" Once all of the Egyptian staff that waited upon Joseph had exited the room, the brothers watch in embarrassed silence as the Egyptian ruler, who earlier had them arrested and brought before him presumably for their sentencing, now breaks down in loud

108

sobbing, crying that was loud enough for the entire court of Pharaoh to hear it.

This moment: awkward, frightening, clumsy, filled with love but also terror. What else can describe this moment? In the Biblical text, the brothers have said nothing in response to Joseph. They stand in terrified silence. Judah and the rest are now at a loss for words. But Joseph "breaks the ice" again by moving toward his precious brother Benjamin, and he "falls" (the literal word here) upon his brother's neck, and he again weeps. Benjamin embraces his long lost brother back and weeps as well. This grand Egyptian ruler is his own brother!

They talk, and I suspect that they talked and talked some more. There are many years of their lives that must now be brought up to date. This day in Joseph's house began with the brothers happily journeying back home, but then that was abruptly halted when they were apprehended and brought back to his house for judgment. Judah had given a moving defense that causes Joseph's rigid facade to crack. The day is now ending with the brothers taking a major step forward toward the unity of this family, a dramatic movement toward reconciliation among brothers. Joseph's actions toward his brothers had been firm and apparently harsh, but the outcome is beautiful in that the issues of recognizing guilt, seeing what grief their sins had caused, realizing that love was costly and demanding, even sacrificial—all that had been brought to the surface by the winnowing process through which Joseph had put his brothers.

If left to ourselves, we would kill each other in a bloodbath of hatred and revenge. When the power and tenderness of God's grace and love take over, there is reunion, unity, healing of the past, and hope for the future. In Genesis 45 we see something of the beauty of God's Kingdom because of the Prince of Peace, Jesus Christ.

Points to Ponder and Discuss

1. Joseph sends all his Egyptian attendants out of the room. In this way they will not hear the disturbing fact that Joseph's brothers were the ones who had sold him into slavery. All they will hear are Joseph's loud sobs coupled with the news that his brothers are now with him. Why does Joseph act so that his family's "dirty laundry" does not get exposed? Does he simply want this moment of revelation to be private and personal?

2. Joseph points out at least these two realities: "You sold me...God sent me." Here we see the realities of God's great sovereignty, on the one hand, and human responsibility, on the other hand. How are both things true in this particular story? Does God's sovereign control of all things excuse the brothers for the guilt of their actions against Joseph?

3. What comfort do we have as believers in a sovereign God that He will work out everything for the good of those who love Him? Is there any comfort in believing in a God who is not completely sovereign? How does "good theology" help Christian believers deal with difficult circumstances in their lives?

4. Read Psalm 133. Joseph forgave his brothers and loved them. This leads to restored unity among the brothers, or, at least, the first important steps toward brothers dwelling in unity. Why is Christian unity so important, and why is it so painful when it is missing? What does Psalm 133 say is God's blessing upon Christian unity? What sinful things disrupt Christian unity today?

5. Joseph's emotional meltdown touches every thoughtful reader who listens to this story with Christian sensitivity. Obviously Joseph was glad to see his brothers and to reveal himself finally to them. Could it be that the brothers were also overjoyed to realize that Joseph was not dead, to know that their murderous hatred had not, in the end, succeeded? Do people act sinfully and foolishly, and then on the "morning after," hope that their sinful acts do not succeed? Do we sometimes "sow wild oats," and then hope for a crop failure?

6. Jesus is Lord of all the earth. He has gone ahead of us to prepare a place for us (see John 14:1ff.). How does Joseph's treatment of his brothers in Genesis 45:1–15 reflect and anticipate how Christ treats those whom His grace has adopted as His brothers and sisters?

Lesson 15

Pharaoh Directs Israel to Move

Read Genesis 45:16–28

Introduction: Reconciliation After Testing
Joseph reveals himself to his stunned brothers. When the
reality dawns upon them that they have been dealing all this
time with their very own brother Joseph, the scene becomes
very emotional. Joseph and Benjamin embrace each other
and weep. The brothers talk together a long time about
many things. Joseph has tested his brothers, and now the
time for family reunion begins. God is good! Though He
may place many trials and tests along the pathway of His
people's lives, in the end He brings about greater blessings.
Joseph has tested his own brothers, and the reconciliation is
a beautiful picture and example of how God's grace can
impact our lives.

Pharaoh Says, "Come on Down!" (45:16–20)
 Earlier in verse 2 it was noted that the report of Joseph's
brothers being "in town" with Joseph had reached the ears
of the Pharaoh. That part of the story had been interrupted
as we read the details of Joseph revealing himself to
his brothers. Verse 16 now picks up that part of the story.
The news reports about Joseph's brothers being in Egypt
could not, of course, be kept from the king of Egypt.
Pharaoh and the entire Egyptian court hear this, and they
are very pleased by this news. Pharaoh is not passive
in his reaction, but he gives very specific directions to
Joseph about transferring the entire extended family
of Joseph from the land of Canaan to Egypt. Carts loaded

with goods are to go to Joseph's father, and the carts can
be used again to transport everything down to Egypt.
An all-expense paid trip to Egypt, one might say!
"Don't worry about a thing," says Pharaoh (verse 20).
"You will be put up in the best region that Egypt has to offer."

Going to Egypt has not been beneficial for the people of
God up to this point. Consider these earlier incidents.
Abram and Sarai nearly met with disaster in Genesis 12:10–20.
The Pharaoh expels them once he realizes that Sarai was in
fact Abram's wife. Then later on in Genesis 26:2 the Lord
warns Isaac not to go to Egypt. But now the conditions
seem to permit entrance into Egypt, even by God's direction.
Yet Israel must remain a distinct (i.e., holy, separate) people
in Egypt. This separation of the covenant people is always
important, in both Canaan and in Egypt.

Here we see that God's plan of salvation is carried
through in spite of evil intentions by men. The focus is not
on Joseph's graciousness and big-heartedness. Yes, he is
gracious and most helpful, but the real focus is going to be
on God's preservation of the covenant race. But it is more
than mere preservation; it is glory and honor.
The Pharaoh assures Joseph and Jacob's family of the
"best that Egypt contains; you will live on the fat of the
land" (verse 18) and "the best of all Egypt is yours"
(verse 20). God has steered the Egyptian king to give
nothing but the best for His people.

Joseph Arranges for the Family Move (45:21–24)

In obedience to Pharaoh's wishes, but especially in a desire
to unite his family in a physical sense, Joseph sets about to
prepare the way for his family to come to Egypt. We are
not surprised to read that he furnishes his brothers with
the necessary supplies for the journey back to Canaan.
Verse 22 tells us that he provides each brother with a
change of clothing. We can understand this on several levels.

Of course, it is a token of his affection to give them clothes.
But is there a bit of irony here as well? After all, it was a
special coat from his father Jacob that had contributed to
the brothers' hatred of Jacob. It was that same coat that
had been stripped from Joseph by the bitter brothers,
dipped in goat's blood and then presented to their father.
Now the tables are turned: it is Joseph who is in charge of
all Egypt, and he hands out the clothes to brothers who had
once taken Joseph's coat away! And his brother Benjamin
gets extra money and more clothes! Donkeys are loaded
with goodies and food. This will not only help them on the
return trip, but these goodies will also be evidence for Jacob
to see that the story is true: Joseph is alive and is doing very
well in Egypt.

There is one more thing that Joseph tells his brothers
before they leave. In verse 24 he says, "Don't quarrel on
the way!" Now it may be possible to understand the words
in the original to mean that they should not be afraid for
their safety while they go back to Canaan. However, most
understand this sentence to mean that Joseph does not want
them to get tangled up in mutual blaming and recriminations.
After all, now everything is out in the open for all to see.
The guilt that had been gnawing away at the consciences of
the brothers—perhaps more for some, less for others—is
now uncovered. They had tried to snuff out Joseph's
existence, but here he is, big as life. Their dirty deeds of the
past now could easily become the reason for a mutual
blame-game. But Joseph appears to say to them, "Don't even
talk about it! There is no profit in that discussion." In other
words, he does not want his brothers to dig up the past and
assign blame for the sinful actions of the past. What is past,
is past! And no one can change the past in the sense of
actually turning the clock backward. Joseph has forgiven
them because he sees the bigger picture, namely, that God
was working to bring about saving his family's lives and

bringing a blessing to many other people in the process.
S.G. De Graaf (*Promise and Deliverance*, vol. 1, p. 240)
says that the brothers were not "to blame themselves or
each other, for the wrongdoing had been erased.
Together with Joseph, they would believe in forgiveness.
In that belief, they would be one." Forgiveness allows
everyone to move on again in life.

Good News Revives a Father's Broken Heart (45:25–28)

We have dealt with the portion of the story that is reported in
Genesis 45:25–28 (see *Bible Studies on Jacob: Genesis 25–49*,
p. 130). Briefly, we simply note that the news of Joseph being still
alive is initially met with unbelief on the part of Jacob. All the
previous years of Joseph being absent had caused Jacob's heart
to run cold and numb with grief, but all the words and evidence
of Egyptian carts mount up to present aged Jacob with a
conclusion that he could not deny. He now accepts the good
news that the son who once was (thought to be) dead, was very
much alive. The news of that "resurrection" (so to speak)
kindled a flame of spiritual comfort for father Jacob.

The thoughtful reader is reminded of our reading of the
Easter morning accounts in the Gospels where the initial
reports of Jesus being alive again, risen from the dead, were
initially met with unbelief. We think of Jesus' disciple
Thomas, who heard the reports of an empty tomb and of a
living Savior, but he would not believe it until he was
confronted with physical evidence (John 20:24ff.). But God
is the God of miracles, of strange possibilities, and of
unbelievable realities. Joseph never physically died, but the
perception was that he had died. They say that "perception
is reality." Well, yes and no. The reality is that Joseph was
alive, although the perception had been—and they all had
believed this!—that Joseph was dead. Jesus Christ, on the
other hand, was really dead when He died on the cross on
Good Friday. That was both the reality and the perception

held by all. But the gospel is good news of what God does for us! Jesus Christ is risen from the dead! That is reality as well, and this wonderful message brings hope and courage, comfort and confidence to God's people who embrace this with faith in the power of the Holy Spirit.

For Jacob and his entire family, a brand new chapter is about to be written. Their night is passing, and a new dawn confronts them with the marvelous reality that Joseph is not dead, but he lives and has great authority over a powerful empire. The thoughtful reader knows that many, many more years must pass before the Kingdom of God will come in power and glory. There will be dramatic setbacks for the people of God in the years ahead. God's covenant people will not always stay on the main track that leads to glory. But a refreshing oasis is being reached for the people of the Lord as these preparations are made for Israel to relocate in Egypt.

Points to Ponder and Discuss

1. What is so striking or noteworthy about Pharaoh's reaction to the news that Joseph's brothers have come to Egypt? Is it somewhat unusual to have Pharaoh actually command that Joseph's family join him in Egypt? What does this suggest about what Pharaoh thinks of Joseph and his presence in Egypt?

2. Pharaoh may or may not be consciously aware that what he is doing for Joseph's family is a part of the divine plan, but Proverbs 21:1 says that the Lord can move the heart of the king as He wills (cf. Dan. 4:31–32, 35; Isaiah 45:1–3). What examples are there today (or in recent history) of how governments and national leaders have acted for the benefit of God's people, the church? What risks are there when Christians begin to rely upon the state and political leaders for benefits and favors?

3. The Spirit of the Christ is working in the heart and life of Joseph. Joseph's actions reflect something of what Christ would do for us later in redemptive history. Read John 14:1–6. Just as Joseph had prepared things for the arrival of his family, what has Christ done to prepare for our arrival in our eternal home, the new creation? In what ways is the Father's house mentioned in John 14:2 so much better than the best of the land of Egypt?

4. God had repeatedly promised the patriarchs Abraham, Isaac, and Jacob the "pillar promises" of land and seed (descendants). Moving out of Canaan puts the promise of land into question, does it not? How relevant is Genesis 15:13–16 to this plan to move Jacob and his family to Egypt? What is good about this move, and what is dangerous about this move?

5. Joseph tells his brothers not to quarrel (Gen. 45:24). How does this reflect the Spirit of the Lord Jesus Christ as His will for life is heard in the words of Joseph? How is the gospel to make an impact on the way this household of God is to live together?

6. Psalm 25:7 asks the Lord God not to remember the "sins of youth." How are sins forgiven? Does God remember those sins? Why or why not? Why is it sometimes hard for us to accept God's forgiveness? What happens when people continue to dwell upon their sins and their guilt?

Lesson 16

Israel Moves to Goshen

Read Genesis 46:28–47:12

Introduction: All Israel Moves

The book of Exodus tells the story of how God brings His people out of Egypt and sets them on the journey toward the Promised Land. The stories in these chapters of Genesis, on the other hand, tell us how Israel comes to dwell in Egypt in the first place. The Joseph-Judah stories in Genesis 37–50 serve as a kind of narrative bridge that carries us over from Canaan to Egypt. Canaan is indeed the Promised Land, but to survive physically, Israel must go down to Egypt for a period of time. God was working in the midst of the sinful actions of Joseph's brothers to prepare the way for Israel to move his entire household to the best part of Egypt, the land of Goshen.

This move was specifically and enthusiastically endorsed by Pharaoh himself. The ruler of Egypt wants Joseph to send for his father and all that belongs to Joseph's family. Joseph puts the services and resources of Egypt to work so that Israel, his entire family (children and grandchildren), and all his possessions might move to Egypt. God will even come to Jacob in a vision of the night (Gen. 46:2–4), and He assures the aging patriarch that this move has heaven's approval. Many things are looking up, one might say.

We get a long list of names in which the inspired text of Genesis 46 tells us who went down to Egypt. The division of family units here is by each wife and her maidservant, Leah with Zilpah, then Rachel with Bilhah. The text tells us

that 70 people went into Egypt, i.e., "all Israel"
(cf. Deut. 10:22). There are some Biblical critics who say
that only some of Israel went to Egypt, only some came out
later, and some never left Canaan at all! But such a view is
not in agreement with the biblical text. Furthermore, the
Greek translation of Exodus 1:5 gives us the number of 75,
not 70. Apparently Stephen quotes this when his words are
recorded in Acts 7:14. Some scholars suggest that this figure
may include five more descendants of Joseph (see the NIV
Study Bible note for Acts 7:14).

In any case, the number 70 may represent a
complete population. Some suggest that the number of
peoples recorded in Genesis 10 comes to 70 nations.
Shem, Ham, and Japheth are the ancestors of the world's
population after the Flood. Admittedly, one can be a little too
imaginative at times about the use of numbers in the Bible.
Yet consider this: Leah's and Zilpah's descendants together
are forty-nine (7 x 7), and Rachel's and Bilhah's descendants
together are twenty-one (3 x 7). So, this deliberate use of the
number 70 (10 x 7) may very well point in the direction
of saying that the family of Jacob is the seedbed of a
new world population. We may not be there yet in
redemptive-history, but God is delivering the family of Jacob,
the people of Israel, so that the Redeemer may come later
through their generational ranks. Through Israel there is the
route to a new community that is (called to be) joined to the
living God, as God's grace joins His elect to Christ, God's Son.

Joseph Meets and Prepares Israel (46:28–34)

Jacob appoints his fourth son Judah to go ahead to Joseph
in order that the final parts of the move might go well.
The rise of Judah to that of the leader among Jacob's sons is
nearly complete (see Gen. 43:3, 8–10; 44:11–34). Jacob is
clearly leaning upon this son Judah and not upon the other
older sons of Leah (Reuben, Simeon, and Levi). Judah had

given the speech that had melted the heart of Joseph such that he had revealed himself to his brothers earlier in Genesis 45. But here is an irony: Judah had been a son that was responsible for actions that had brought Joseph to Egypt. Now he is the son who is made responsible for bringing Israel and his entire household into Egypt. Judah sees to it that there is a smooth transition into the good land of Goshen.

It is noted by scholars that the name *Goshen* has not been identified as Egyptian, and its precise location in Egypt is not certain. It is likely a Semitic name, and the probable location is in the northeast portion of the Nile River delta. If this is so, then these were certainly excellent areas for raising cattle that could graze in the area. This area was very close to the frontier border of Egypt in the northeast, and it probably was not that far distant from where Joseph lived in the royal court (see Gen. 45:10 and 47:1ff.).

When Joseph finally sees his aged father again, we read again of a very touching and emotional scene of embracing and prolonged weeping. Father Jacob had loved Joseph more than his other sons, and Jacob had provided his favorite son with a special coat that suggested royal appointment. Joseph knew that his father loved him, and both of them are deeply moved at the moment of meeting again after so many years of separation. God's goodness is seen here in that a divine plan works to unite this family again for greater purposes in God's Kingdom. These have been very difficult years, and the moral choices of Jacob's sons have not been stellar. Yet in Christ, things will work out for the good of God's people in the end. This is our Christian faith, our confession, because this is what God reveals to us (see Rom. 8:28–39).

Israel says that he is ready to die because he has seen his son alive. Again, our thoughts are drawn to the New Testament's revelation where we read of Simeon who can now leave this life in peace because his eyes have actually seen the Lord's Christ (see Luke 2:29–32).

Joseph now prepares his family so that they are properly rehearsed when he presents them to Pharaoh. They are told to indicate that their occupation is that of caring for livestock, since the Egyptians abhor shepherds (verse 34; cf. Gen. 43:32). Such abhorrence about shepherds would not remain only something that afflicted the Egyptians. Later on in history the Jews would also look down on shepherds. In the first century A.D. we are told that shepherds could not give testimony in the courts of the land since their word was not viewed as trustworthy. Yet it is to lowly shepherds that angels come in Luke 2:8ff. to announce the birth of Christ the Lord. For He is the Savior of His people, all His people, and such people can be found in every area of society, in every economic class, in every culture and tribe, and in every corner of the world. This is good news! In Christ there is neither Jew nor Gentile, there is neither slave nor free, there is neither male nor female (Gal. 3:28). Therefore, God's people do not look down on anyone as unclean or unworthy of receiving the good news.

Joseph Presents His Family to Pharaoh (47:1–6)

The moment arrives, and the family of Joseph comes before the great king of Egypt. Pharaoh is told that everyone and everything has come to Goshen. It is interesting to note that Joseph had said that he would tell Pharaoh what line of work his family was engaged in, but he leaves that all somewhat vague in his actual remarks to Pharaoh. He is somewhat indirect when he says that his family, their "flocks and herds" are here. Thus Pharaoh asks them what their occupation is, and they respond, "We are shepherds and always have been. Now, may we live in Goshen?" Pharaoh not only agrees, but he even asks them for help with his own royal livestock!

Jacob Blesses Pharaoh (47:7–10)

There are some Old Testament scholars who see the idea of as one of the key themes that runs throughout the book of Genesis. In the beginning God blesses the creatures that He has made as well as mankind whom He makes in His image. Blessing is something that Abram is promised, and through him all the families of the earth will be blessed (Gen. 12:1–3). Blessing is something that comes to God's people from God in order that they in turn might be a blessing to others. The Lord is our light and salvation (Ps. 27:1), and Jesus is the Light of the world (John 8:12), but we in turn are called, in union with Christ, to be the light of this world (Matt. 5:14).

Jacob "blesses" Pharaoh when he meets him and as he leaves him (verses 7 and 10). To be sure, the word in the original can have the meaning of "greet." But that action of Jacob has a powerful sound to us who read it. This aged man is blessing the man whom the Egyptians revered as a living god! This is amazing.

Jacob is 130 years old. He would live another seventeen years in the land of Egypt before the Lord calls him from this life. We are struck by his description of his age as being a "few days" (verse 9). His grandfather Abraham died at age 175 years, and his father Isaac died at age 180 years. Jacob seems to say that by comparison, he has lived only a "few days" when he considers the life spans of his father and grandfather. Today, however, people who live to be 130 years old would make the headlines! When such long-lived folks pass away, there is usually a notice of such passing in the news. Psalm 90:10 says that our days are normally 70 or maybe 80 years.

But Jacob adds another descriptive term to describe his "few days." He says that they have been "difficult." The term in the original can mean "miserable, troubled, evil." Jacob has often talked about dying, about going down to

Sheol, the realm of the dead (see Gen. 37:35; 42:38; 44:29–31). One gets the impression that life has become a great burden to Jacob, and he would sooner leave this life and its miseries. In fact, now that his eyes have actually beheld his beloved Joseph, he can die and leave this "vale of tears."

Joseph Provides Land and Bread (47:11,12)

These two verses give us a summary of Joseph carrying out the command of Pharaoh. Pharaoh wants Joseph's family to have the best of the land. Joseph's family settles in the choice district of "Rameses," called the "best of the land" (verses 6 and 11). This name has provoked much discussion since the first known Pharaoh with the name Rameses comes later than the time of Joseph. Some explain that it is an anachronistic explanation to help the later readers understand where the region is, since the Ramesside dynasty began its rule in 1319 B.C. There is now some evidence to suggest that the name "Rameses" is earlier than the dynasty so-named. Future discoveries may throw more light on the use of the name Rameses. In any case, Israel is now in Egypt, there to experience God's providence in both goodness and affliction later on in this foreign land.

Points to Ponder and Discuss

1. Speculate just a little bit. Is it likely that Jacob's family (the people of Israel) knew of the story of Abram and Sarai being expelled earlier (see Gen. 12:10–20)? Could they be aware that Isaac was told not to go to Egypt (see Gen. 26:2)? Hasn't God been communicating to them that it is best to stay out of Egypt? Why does Joseph (and Pharaoh) want Jacob and his family to come to Egypt so strongly? Why not just send a steady supply of food to Canaan until the famine is over?

2. The Egyptians detested shepherds, and yet the angel of the Lord and a heavenly choir announced Christ's birth to shepherds. Why do some people, or some cultures, look down on some occupations? Is some work "below our dignity," something we leave for cheap labor to perform? If an occupation is legitimate in God's sight, can it serve in some way in the Kingdom of God? Or is our work done Monday through Saturday just "a job" in the "secular world"?

3. God's people will always hear these words when they read this story, "Jacob blessed Pharaoh." If it is true that the greater blesses the lesser (Heb. 7:6, 7; cf. Gen. 14:19), what does this story suggest about Jacob and Pharaoh? How has Joseph already been a blessing to Egypt? Do God's people bring (more) blessings to Egypt and the Egyptian people? Today, how can God's people bring blessings to those who rule us? How is Christ alone the source of blessing to all rulers and to all the peoples of the earth?

4. Paul tells the Philippian Christians that to live is Christ, but to die is gain (Phil. 1:21ff.). Jacob feels ready to die, having sojourned on this earth in the land of Canaan. Christians are pilgrims in this world. Describe the Christian attitude to this life and this world, and the attitude toward leaving this life and world to be with Christ. How do we keep a proper balance?

5. Jacob describes his years as "few and difficult." Is not his age—130 years—a testimony to the faithfulness of God? The older we get, the faster the years seem to go by: "time flies." Why is that? As Christians, we are brought by Christ into the age to come, even while we live in the present. What does it mean that we are to redeem the time, for the days are evil (see Eph. 5:15)?

Joseph Feeds Egypt

Read Genesis 47:13–31

Introduction

Genesis 46:1–47:12 are a kind of narrative bridge between the lands of Canaan and Egypt for Jacob and his clan. He and all his family have entered the land of Egypt. Jacob in fact had an audience with the king of Egypt, Pharaoh himself! Joseph has done his best to see to it that his family would be adequately cared for, and Pharaoh assures this family that the best of the land, the region of Goshen, would be reserved for them. The providence of God is clearly evident in all this since the famine is not yet over. More lean years lie ahead, but the covenant-keeping God has arranged everything for the good of His chosen people. A new chapter of the 'good news' is about to be written, even if it means that darker days lie ahead. In time, a new Pharaoh would arise who would not know or have any memory of the man Joseph and all that he did for Egypt.

A Continuing Food Crisis (47:13–19)

When Joseph had revealed himself to his brothers, two years of famine had passed. There were five more hungry years ahead. Such a famine could only get worse as available food sources and food reserves start to get depleted in the regions where the famine is hitting the hardest. Egypt has food stored up because of the gracious revelation of God and the wise leadership of Joseph. But both Egypt and Canaan are suffering, and it did not get easier for them.

People kept dipping into their cash sources to come up with the means by which they could buy food. In time, all cash resources would be exhausted as people reached deeper into their pockets to find the wherewithal to obtain food.

Since Joseph could not count on a cash income from these hungry people, he then asks for their livestock, which they also use to get food. Here is the first mention of horses, an animal that the Egyptians would master and even sell to others. Solomon later acquired horses from the Egyptians (1 Kings 10:28–29), something that is forbidden to God's chosen king (see Deut. 17:14ff.), since the horse was often used as an animal of war and power, whereas Israel's power and strength were to come from the LORD alone.

Joseph led the Egyptian people through that next famine year. The word used in verse 17 is reminiscent of the actions of a shepherd who cared for a flock. His leadership gave stability to the population during this time of economic crisis.

But the famine dragged on, and elements that could be bartered for food continued to dwindle. The Egyptians stood before Joseph with empty pockets. "The only thing that we have left is our bodies and our land," they say (verse 18). The hungry people willingly give up their property and their persons in order to eat. When actual starvation is staring a person in the face, that person will resort to some desperate measures in order to eat. The Egyptian population sell themselves to Pharaoh; they obtain seed in order to keep planting every year in the hope that the coming year will be better than the last one. In other words, the Egyptians have now become economic serfs, a state of existence somewhere between outright slavery and freedom. Desperate times call for desperate measures...or do they?

Pharaoh Owns Egypt (47:20–22)

The result of Joseph's actions in the light of this ongoing famine is that Pharaoh acquires under his control the entire land of Egypt. Since the government in the person of Joseph had a monopoly on food stuffs—and people have to eat, after all—now this stark reality confronts the Egyptians: you can eat from the hand of the state, but you have no more (economic) freedom. The one exception to this plan is the land of the Egyptian priests. Perhaps the power of Egyptian priests was something that was best left undisturbed. The priests were known in Egyptian history to have been supported by Pharaoh through gifts of food (grain) given to the temples. Egyptian temples owned their own land.

Verse 21 differs in the several English translations, depending on whether they follow the Hebrew text or the Greek Old Testament (Septuagint) text. The NIV says that Joseph reduced the people to servitude, while the Hebrew text says that he moved them to the cities. If the latter is the proper reading, it may be for the purpose of moving farmers off national lands, "or to get them to work other national lands, or to bring them to the city to work on national building projects" (Currid, *Genesis*, 2:357). The storehouses of food existed in the cities. In any case, either action suggests that fairly significant social disruption occurred during this famine, and Joseph is the government leader who plays a large role in all this. We might think of similar social disruptions in the last century. During the "dust bowl" years of the Great Depression, many Midwesterners moved to California. Much more tragically, when communists took over Russia and China, many landowners were removed from their property, many of them killed. Crises can lead to significant changes in society.

Taxes at 20% (47:23–26)

Even in dry years, farmers plant in the hope that things may improve. Joseph knows how long the famine will last, but this does not mean that such insight was common knowledge among all the Egyptian people. Some people continued to work the land, and whatever crops did grow, Joseph took 20% as the share of the government; the rest belonged to the people so that the families and households of Egypt could eat.

The people's response is interesting. The old adage is true: a person does not bite the hand that feeds him. To Joseph comes the loyalty of the Egyptian people. "You have saved our lives!" (verse 25). "Now we belong to Pharaoh." Joseph had acquired the Egyptian people and their land for Pharaoh. The two means of (capital) production have now effectively come under the control of the Egyptian state, for better... or for worse. Gold and grain do not have intrinsic value; their value is whatever people give to it. What lesson is embedded in these events that God's people need to learn today?

"Carry Me Back to Old Canaan" (47:27–31)

On the other hand, verse 27 describes Israel's life in the Goshen region of Egypt. They obtain property as they continue to live there as resident aliens, and their numbers continue to increase. This verse is a kind of literary "oasis" in the sense that the gloom and doom situation that has struck Egypt is contrasted to the bright prospects that the Israelites experience in Goshen. Egyptian land goes to Pharaoh; Israelites acquire property in Goshen.
The Egyptians are desperate to secure food sources; the Israelites begin to grow in number (i.e., they prosper).

This last item is a fulfillment, in part, of what God had repeatedly said to Abraham, Isaac, and Jacob before (e.g., Gen. 12:1–3; 35:11–12). God was certainly

blessing them. But God's people, the church, are not to
remain in Egypt. The reason is not because Egypt is
bad land. Rather, it is not the land of the older covenant
era, promised by the LORD on oath. Yet, while they are
in Egypt, at this moment in time the God of the covenant
is faithful to His promises, and everything that His people
need are provided. God's primary concern is always for
the well-being of His own. In adopting His children,
He will never neglect them, and that is evident also at
this moment in redemptive-history, through the ministry
of Joseph.

And yet...Egypt the country and Goshen the district are
not the homeland. This is not the Promised Land, even if
these were the years of economic boom and plenty.
God's Word is decisive here: He had planted in the hearts
and minds of Jacob and Joseph as well this truth, that God
would establish His own people in a particular place in
the world. When that truth is embrace by faith, it causes all
priorities and every plan to be arranged in such a way that
moves us toward what that truth entails. Canaan is the
Promised Land, while Egypt is not. Thus when Jacob's
remaining seventeen years of life come to an end, he makes
Joseph swear to him that Jacob's body would not lie buried
in Egypt, but rather that Joseph would see to it that Jacob's
body would be returned to the land that the LORD had
promised on oath to give to the children of Abraham.
Jacob's eyes of faith see God's promises, and therefore even
where his dead body lies must be in accord with the
promises of God. "Swear this to me," says Jacob to Joseph.
This Joseph does by placing his hand under his father's
thigh, near the organ of procreation, perhaps to represent
his connection to his family and this solemn obligation to
fulfill his promise. In this way both Jacob, who wants the
oath, and Joseph, who swears the oath, testify to their living
faith that directs their entire being to movement to the place

that God says is home. Canaan, not Egypt, is the
Promised Land.

The same is always true for the people of God today.
We are not our own because we have been bought by the
precious blood of Jesus Christ. Therefore, our only comfort
in life but also in death is that we belong to Him.
For Jacob and for Joseph later on, this means that they
want the resting place for their bones and body to be in the
Promised Land. Christ rested in the grave for us, but He
arose again, and then He moves on to prepare a place for
all believers in the new creation. Because we are raised with
Christ, we too direct our lives, thoughts and actions,
toward that great reality (see Col. 3:1ff.). Our lives belong
to Christ here and now, in every area of life, but our
citizenship is in heaven (Phil. 3:20a).

Points to Ponder and Discuss

1. "His mercies are new every morning; great is
   Thy faithfulness!" How was this true for the children
   of Israel during these famine years?
2. How has the grace of God changed and matured the
   man Judah? Contrast him in his earlier years, as we meet
   him in the text of Scripture, to that point where the
   family of Jacob settles in Goshen in the land of Egypt.
3. Children are dependent upon their parents for food,
   clothing, and protection—the basic necessities of life.
   Young children are, of course, immature. As we mature
   and grow up, we become increasingly responsible for
   providing those things for ourselves. What is the role of
   the community (church? state? family and friends?)
   when we experience genuine needs and shortfalls?

4. Are Joseph's actions of centralizing (economic) power under Pharaoh (the "state") something for that time only, or is this a model (example) for all times?
5. What does this passage remind us of regarding trusting in riches (in money, in property, etc.)? Can we look to the state to supply all our needs? What did our Lord Jesus say in Matthew 6 about our anxiety concerning food and clothing?
6. In Genesis 15:13–14, God had told Abram that his descendants would be afflicted in a foreign land for 400 years, that is, they would be slaves in Egypt. Do Joseph's actions here set things up that help contribute to the Pharaoh's later abuse of the Israelites? What happens when power is centralized and rulers love to have that power?

Final Reconciliation and Future Resolution

Read Genesis 50

Introduction

We have come to the end of this chapter of redemptive-history. God has shown His covenant goodness throughout the life of the great patriarch Jacob. He dies at the age of 147 years (Gen. 47:28), a ripe age by today's standards, although it is several decades briefer than his father Isaac (180 years) and grandfather Abraham (175 years).

Embalming Jacob and Burial in Canaan (50:1–14)

Genesis 49:33 ends that chapter with the notice that Jacob concluded his life in a dignified, almost grand, manner. He has spoken to his sons, noting that he was about "to be gathered to [his] people" (Gen. 49:29). The chapter ends with the Jacob's words of faith in God's promises. He had gathered his sons around him to receive his parting blessing, and now he is gathered to his people in death. Does this suggest that in death he was gathered to the saints of God who had passed out of this life to be with the Lord? After all, the Triune God is the God of the living, not of the dead (Luke 20:38).

Joseph directs his private physicians to embalm the body of his father Jacob. John Currid (*Genesis*, 2:389, 390) says that embalming had become an involved process during the Egyptian Middle Kingdom (ca. 2040–1640 B.C.). The Egyptians were fascinated with death and the possibilities of life after death. In embalming, the internal organs were removed, stored in jars, and the body cavity was packed with a salt to dry out the body. The skin was also treated with resin and spices, and then the body was wrapped in linen strips, placed in a wooden coffin.

The whole process continued to be improved over time in Egypt. Some mummified bodies could be relatively well-kept, as any Egypt section of a museum can attest. The Bible mentions only Jacob and Joseph as children of Abraham who were embalmed. It should also be noted that the Jews did not embalm. When the women were bringing spices to Jesus' tomb on Resurrection morning, it was to give a pleasant smell to a body that would have begun to decay after death. Once all the flesh had decayed, then the bones of the (wealthy) deceased would have been collected into special boxes.

Jacob is taken in grand style and buried by his family in Canaan at the cave in the field of Machpelah, east of Mamre. Others of his family are buried there in the hope of the promise being realized.

"Now We're Going to Get it!" (50:15–21)

With the death of the great patriarch Jacob, the old wounds are activated in the minds of the sons of Jacob. They are now afraid that it is "pay-back time!" Joseph, they fear, may have waited and waited for the moment when his father would die, and then he would strike back in all his fury against his brothers. Esau had plotted just such action in Genesis 27:41. Esau planned to kill Jacob, but he did not want to carry out the foul deed as long as his father Isaac remained alive. Joseph's brothers suspect that their powerful brother Joseph was secretly planning some kind of retaliation against them once father Jacob was dead and gone.

The brothers send a message to Joseph to tell him of a message that reportedly father Jacob had left before his own death. Did Jacob in fact leave such a message, or is this a "white lie" intended to keep Joseph from carrying out any intended vengeance? In any case, they are asking for forgiveness, even if the request is through the intermediary person, father Jacob. This request pains the heart and soul of Joseph, so that again he weeps. In his mind, his brothers had not fully believed his words and actions of forgiveness in Genesis 45 onward.

Here come the brothers again, and they again bow in utter submission to Joseph. His dreams when he was 17 years old continue to come true: the members of his family bow down before him. That bowing stretches from Genesis 37 through Genesis 50. But Joseph basically repeats his earlier message that he gave in Genesis 45: the brothers' motives and actions were evil, intended to kill Joseph. But God! That simple phrase is the great turnaround that lies at the heart of the gospel message. But God, who is rich in mercy, is still sovereign over all the motives and actions of people in this world. He worked through their evil to cause many people, Israelites as well as many others, to live. So, Joseph has to say twice in verses 19–21, "Don't be afraid." That message still echoes today whenever the true gospel is preached, "Don't be afraid!" We are sinners, worthy of death, but Christ has died in our place, and He now lives and reigns in glory. He will provide us with everything we need to live for Him.

Dying With Eyes (of Faith) Wide Open (50:22–26)

Joseph died at the age of 110 years. The Egyptians believed that number was significant: for them it was the ideal length of life. This many years of life enabled Joseph to live long enough to see his grandchildren and even his great-grandchildren. Joseph's sons, Manasseh and Ephraim, were adopted by Jacob (with Ephraim designated to become the "firstborn" in rank). Joseph's grandson, Makir, is named; he is the ancestor of the important Gileadite branch of the Manasseh tribe (cf. Joshua 17:1; Judges 5:14). Verse 23 says that Makir's children were "placed on Joseph's knees," perhaps a reference to Joseph adopting them as his very own.

Joseph has acted in a royal capacity during much of his time in Egypt. But he also acts as a prophet in that he reminds his brothers of the covenant promises of God. Thus he can "see," as it were, into the future. He tells his brothers of what God is going to do later on the basis of what God has said earlier. "God will surely come to your aid." Here again is God-given faith in the Word. We know what God has said. Believing that enables us to speak, even about future events, although we might not know the particular details.

Joseph has lived most of his life in Egypt, and most of those years (after his imprisonment) were lived in a position of power and relative comfort. He had become one of the highest officials in the land of Egypt! His wife was an Egyptian from an important section of society. Humanly speaking, Joseph had it made! But that did not count a great deal to Joseph. He had come to know the promise of God, and he embraced that promise so that when his earthly journey would end, his bones (his body) would rest in Egypt, but only for a time. Joseph also believed that the day would come when the church, the community of people that were gathered by the Word of the LORD, would leave the land of Egypt, and this family of faith would journey back to Canaan. Egypt may have many physical pleasures, but it is not "home." With all of its advantages, pleasures and power, Egypt is still an alien land to those whose lives are gripped by the word of God's promise. By faith, Joseph also wants his bones to rest

(until the resurrection) not in Egypt but in Canaan
(see Heb. 11:22). God's Word always informs our faith,
and then our spiritual eyes are directed to look where they
should look. This present world is not our permanent home.
We await the new creation in the firm resolve of faith.

Joseph's Significance

What is the significance of this man Joseph in the history
of redemption? On the historical road back to the face of
God, on the way back to Paradise, the people of God had
been detoured to Egypt, as earlier with Abram. The reason
is famine again (cf. Gen 12:10–20). But before the clan of
Jacob goes down to Egypt, one of the family goes ahead of
the others. He is sold, sent away (in his brothers' minds)
to death. But in God's plan, Joseph goes to prepare a place
for them. He came on the command of the father to check
on their welfare (their *shalom*), but they hated him and
plotted against him. "He came unto his own, but his own
would not receive him." How many things in Joseph's life
anticipate the Lord Jesus Christ! Joseph was "attacked"
by his brothers but also by a Gentile's lies, those of
Potiphar's wife. He experiences both humiliation and
exaltation, being nearly "cut off from the land of the living"
(cf. Isaiah 53:8b and Phil. 2:8–9). But in the end, we wears
the royal robe, serving as a royal protector and provider for
His people but also for many people of the world.

Truly there is much in the person, life, and ministry of
Joseph that is analogous to, even typical of, the person, life,
and ministry of our Savior and Lord, Jesus Christ.
Commentators frequently note this (see, for example, Dr. G.
Van Groningen, *Messianic Revelation in the Old Testament*,
p. 166). All of this is an unfolding of God's plan for
delivering His people alive, always in the midst of threats.
The Satanic dragon-lion is always trying to attack the
mother who is great with Child in the old covenant era,

as Revelation 12 reminds us. But God always provides a
way of escape. This is what Joseph sees and understands,
and his revelation provides not only a perspective on
events, even evil events, it contributes to the attitude of
forgiveness and acceptance on the part of the one who
is wronged. By God's grace, Joseph sees God's hand in all
these things. He can forgive his brothers all the evil that they
have plotted.

Joseph's life work in Egypt has several different points of focus:

1. He reveals God's will to both the church (community
   of faith) and the world. Here is the pattern: dreams
   come from God (revelation), he interprets them
   (e.g., Gen. 41:39–40), which in turn leads to exaltation
   (eventually), power and honor.

2. He is able to feed God's people but also the "whole earth."
   Thus blessing is coming to many nations through the seed
   of Abraham (cf. Gen. 12:3). This is the first real instance of
   this thing on a somewhat large scale. This looks ahead to
   what Psalm 72 will say about the Messianic king: when the
   needy look to Him, He will feed them.

3. Joseph sifts the church by searching out the hearts and
   motives of his brothers. If he had hated them and sought
   strict justice, he could have had his brothers killed at the
   first meeting. Had he been only indulgent, he might have
   revealed himself right away at the first meeting, told
   them "all is forgiven," and invited them to come on
   down ("cheap grace"). He does not do either. Rather, he
   engages in a kind of "cat and mouse" game with them to
   see what really lived in their hearts after all those years.
   It is in this back and forth struggle that Judah emerges as
   pre-eminent among his brothers.

4. There is a focal point of separation. This is perhaps more
   subtle, but it appears to be present. This has already been
   seen in the life-partners chosen for the patriarchs Isaac
   (Rebekah) and Jacob (Leah and Rachel). Esau had married

two Hittites and an Ishmaelite, while Judah married a Canaanite (Gen. 38). Jacob and his clan will live separated lives in Egypt. Joseph, in faith, will separate his bones in death so that they may some day rest in the Promised Land of Canaan.

Points to Ponder and Discuss

1. In what ways did the LORD God mature Jacob and strengthen his faith over the years?
2. Review briefly the life of Joseph. How did the LORD God mature him and sanctify him in his life?
3. Why do the brothers find it so hard to believe that Joseph has really forgiven them? Do some Christians today also have a difficult time believing that God is truly gracious to us in Christ?
4. Genesis 50:26, the last verse of the book of Genesis, names Joseph, his age at death, the embalming of his body, and his placement in a coffin. This is a rather sober, almost chilly, ending to the story. Yet, why is this not the last word to the story? How is death never the last word for God's people in Jesus Christ?
5. Joseph served in the court of a foreign king and contributed to the benefit of God's people. How would Daniel and Esther later on do similar kinds of things in the court of the Babylonian and Persian kings?
6. When Joseph tells his brothers about the future, it is not on the basis of some vision or dream. He simply reminds them of what God has promised to do. What can Christians today say, on the basis of God's Word, about the future? What is going to happen in the future in history and at the end of history? What is going to happen to the church communally and to all believers personally?

Notes

Notes

Notes

Notes